Executive Policing

Enforcing the Law in Peace
Operations

sipri

Stockholm International Peace Research Institute
Signalistgatan 9, SE-169 70 Solna, Sweden
Cable: SIPRI
Telephone: 46 8/655 97 00
Telefax: 46 8/655 97 33
Email: sipri@sipri.org
Internet URL: http://www.sipri.org

Executive Policing

Enforcing the Law in Peace Operations

SIPRI Research Report No. 16

Edited by
Renata Dwan

OXFORD UNIVERSITY PRESS
2002

OXFORD
UNIVERSITY PRESS

Great Clarendon Street, Oxford OX2 6DP
Oxford University Press is a department of the University of Oxford.
It furthers the University's objective of excellence in research, scholarship,
and education by publishing worldwide in

Oxford New York
Auckland Bangkok Buenos Aires Cape Town Chennai
Dar es Salaam Delhi Hong Kong Istanbul Karachi Kolkata
Kuala Lumpur Madrid Melbourne Mexico City Mumbai Nairobi
São Paulo Shanghai Taipei Tokyo Toronto

Oxford is a registered trade mark of Oxford University Press
in the UK and certain other countries

Published in the United States
by Oxford University Press Inc., New York

British Library Cataloguing in Publication Data
Data available

Library of Congress Cataloguing-in-Publication Data
Data available

ISBN 0-19-925824-4
ISBN 0-19-926267-5 (*pbk*)

Typeset and originated by Stockholm International Peace Research Institute
Printed in Great Britain on acid-free paper by
Biddles Ltd., Guildford and King's Lynn

Contents

Preface

This report is the result of a study designed and led by Dr Renata Dwan, leader of the Stockholm International Peace Research Institute (SIPRI) Project on Conflict Prevention, Management and Resolution. International policing as a subject of research is new, both in theory and in practice. The end of the cold war brought about profound changes to the nature and practice of international peacekeeping. International peace operations have expanded from a discrete and limited set of tasks—monitoring and confirming the observance of ceasefires between conflicting states—to include assistance in making, enforcing, maintaining and building peace within states. In 1999, a new Rubicon was crossed when the United Nations assumed authority to administer the transition from war to sustainable peace in two regions—Kosovo in the Federal Republic of Yugoslavia and East Timor, a former colony of Portugal, occupied by Indonesia since 1975. UN rule is intended to fundamentally transform the status of these two entities, in the case of East Timor to sovereign statehood and in Kosovo, less unanimously, to substantial autonomy.

The consequences of the assumption of executive authority by UN peace operations are only now beginning to emerge. One of the most immediate is the crucial role played by international police in efforts to restore and (re)build stable societies. Between the autumn of 2000 and the spring of 2002, SIPRI undertook a project—International Policing: The New Agenda—to explore this particular dimension of peace operations. The project looked at the way in which the expansion of international engagement in intra-state conflicts has focused attention on the rule of law as the foundation for order and stability within societies. The actors, the policies and the tools which are being developed to help establish the sustainable rule of law in societies emerging from conflict have been the focus of the SIPRI study.

Some of the findings are reflected in this report. It examines the issue of law enforcement by international police forces—a question that Kosovo and East Timor have forced the international community to address formally for the first time. Six authors with diverse professional backgrounds have contributed chapters which examine particular aspects of this challenge and how they might be addressed in the light of experiences in Kosovo and East Timor.

Many people assisted in the preparation of this volume. Our thanks go to Renata Dwan and to the contributing authors for their cooperation and diligence. Special thanks are due to SIPRI research assistant Sharon Wiharta, who undertook background research, and SIPRI editor Eve Johansson, who prepared the manuscript for publication.

Funding was generously provided by the Ministry for Justice, Equality and Law Reform of Ireland and the Ministry of Foreign Affairs of Sweden. SIPRI would like to express its gratitude to the Irish and Swedish governments for their willingness to support innovative policy-oriented research.

Adam Daniel Rotfeld
Director, SIPRI
May 2002

Alyson J. K. Bailes
Director, SIPRI
September 2002

Acronyms and abbreviations

CivPol — Civilian police
CIU — Criminal Intelligence Unit (UNMIK)
CPU — Close Protection Unit (UNMIK)
DPKO — Department of Peace-keeping Operations (UN)
ETPS — East Timorese Police Service
ETPTC — East Timor Police Training College
EU — European Union
FRY — Federal Republic of Yugoslavia
FTO — Field Training Officer
ICITAP — International Criminal Investigative Training Assistance Program (US Department of Justice)
INTERFET — International Force for East Timor
IPTF — International Police Task Force (Bosnia and Herzegovina)
JIAS — Joint Interim Administrative Structure (Kosovo)
KFOR — Kosovo Force
KLA — Kosovo Liberation Army
KPC — Kosovo Protection Corps
KPS — Kosovo Police Service
KPSS — Kosovo Police Service School
LDK — Democratic League of Kosovo
MNF — Multi-national Force (Haiti)
MSU — Multinational Specialized Unit
NATO — North Atlantic Treaty Organization
NGO — Non-governmental organization
OSCE — Organization for Security and Co-operation in Europe
PAG — Police Assistance Group (East Timor)
ROE — Rules of engagement
SFOR — Stabilization Force
SPU — Special Police Unit (UNMIK)
UNDP — United Nations Development Programme
UNMIK — UN Interim Administration Mission in Kosovo
UNTAET — UN Transitional Administration in East Timor

1. Introduction

Renata Dwan

I. What is executive policing?

'Executive policing' is the newest term to enter the lexicon of United Nations peacekeeping. The phrase has come into use in diplomatic and international policing circles only since the establishment of the UN Interim Administration Mission in Kosovo (UNMIK) in June 1999 following the intervention by the North Atlantic Treaty Organization (NATO) in the Federal Republic of Yugoslavia (FRY). Like much of the terminology of peacekeeping, executive policing is a specialized term. What is executive policing? How does it differ from any other type of policing? Where and when does it happen?

Unlike much peacekeeping jargon, executive policing is a fairly precise concept. It refers to the power and practice of law enforcement by international police within a particular territory. This power derives from the assumption by the UN of sovereign authority over the area (either all or part of a state) and its practice from the establishment of a transitional administration. To date, UNMIK and the UN Transitional Administration in East Timor (UNTAET), established in October 1999, are the only two examples of executive policing in a peace operation. There are at least three reasons why so few executive policing operations have been established. These reasons also point to some of the distinguishing characteristics of the phenomenon.

The first is respect for the principle of sovereignty on which the international system of states has been based. The cornerstone of the sovereign state is its legitimate monopoly of coercive power within its territorial boundaries. This internal supremacy rests in no small degree on the external sovereignty of the state—its independence from outside authorities.[1] The maintenance of internal law and order, in this context, is considered the responsibility of each individual state, to be pursued without interference by external actors. This understanding of sovereignty has dominated the way in which relations between states are conducted. According to the UN Department of Peace-keeping

---

[1] See, e.g., Bull, H., *The Anarchical Society: A Study of Order in World Politics* (Macmillan: London, 1977).

Operations (DPKO), for example, the UN Security Council would only mandate a UN peace operation to assume such broad powers in areas where there is a near-vacuum in civil authority.[2]

In such a context, the police component of the international administration is called upon, as the European Union (EU) describes it, to substitute for local police forces.[3] The restricted conditions under which executive policing can be undertaken, according to the UN and the EU, illustrate the sensitivity of international law enforcement for the principle of sovereignty. International police law enforcement can only take place within the context of a UN Security Council-mandated peace operation.

A second reason why there have been so few instances of executive policing is its feasibility. The assumption of responsibility for law enforcement in a mission area has major practical consequences for the police component of an international peace operation. Under this authority international police are accountable for all aspects of law enforcement in a society, from traffic offences to criminal investigations to riot control. Their tasks, as in their home countries, are to provide security, deter crime, protect life and property, and pursue challenges to public order. They must perform these functions in countries with which they often have little or no familiarity and under conditions that are, by definition, extremely difficult, such as the absence or insufficiency of applicable law and local resentment of their presence.

The responsibility requires significant numbers of international police personnel with wide-ranging skills and experience. Such personnel are already in short supply in many Western states and, given the increasing dominance of crime and public order issues in domestic politics in Europe and North America, in demand in their home countries. The personnel and financial implications of executive policing for international institutions and contributing states are therefore domestic as well as international political issues. Only in exceptional, emergency situations will states be convinced that it is in their interest to submit their own domestic order to further pressure in order to take on the burdens of the internal order of another state.

---

[2] United Nations, Department of Peace-keeping Operations, *United Nations Civilian Police Principles and Guidelines* (UN: New York, 2001), p. 6.

[3] European Union, 'Presidency Report on the European Security and Defence Policy, European Council, Nice, 7–9 December 2000', annex II to annex VI, 'Strengthening of European Union capabilities for civilian aspects of crisis management'.

This points to a second key element of the concept of executive policing: it is a temporary, short-term measure taken by the international community to plug a serious domestic security gap.

A third, related, factor behind the lack of executive policing to date is the way in which international policing in peace operations has been carried out. Although the first instance of a police component forming part of a peace operation—the UN Operation in the Congo (ONUC) in 1964–65—occurred four decades ago, international civilian police (CivPols) became a significant element in UN peace-keeping only at the end of the 1980s.[4] The 1500 police in the UN Transition Assistance Group (UNTAG) in Namibia in 1989 set the framework for CivPol operations—observing and monitoring local police as they carried out their law enforcement duties, with particular attention to their respect for human rights. Subsequent operations saw the evolution of CivPol tasks to include advising local police on law enforcement practices and standards, and training local officers in them. By 1995 these tasks were encapsulated by the DPKO in the 'SMART' concept—Supporting human rights; Monitoring the performance of the local enforcement authority; Advising the local police on best practice; Reporting on situations and incidents; and Training local enforcement in best practice for policing and human rights. The pressures on the small DPKO Civilian Police Unit and the tendency to appoint senior police personnel from a previous mission to lead new operations meant that the SMART concept remained rather static and dominated thinking on international policing. It was applied without significant rethinking in diverse peace missions in Africa, Asia, Europe and Latin America during the 1990s: SMART tasks were still recognized as the core of international policing when the war in Kosovo began in 1999.[5]

Responsibility for the rule of law sets executive policing apart from the previous model of international policing and gives it a number of particular characteristics. First, international police officers in an executive police mission have the power to arrest and detain individuals and to investigate crimes of all kinds. Second, they are armed, a reflection of the fact that they carry out their policing functions in an unstable environment of tension, if not actual conflict. Third, the

---

[4] For a historical overview see Schmidl, E. A., 'Police in peace operations', *Informationen zur Sicherheitspolitik* (Landesverteidigungsakademie, Vienna), no. 10 (Sep. 1998).

[5] See, e.g., Hartz, H., 'CIVPOL: the UN instrument for police reform', *International Peacekeeping*, vol. 6, no. 4 (winter 1999), pp. 27–42.

international police force carries out its law enforcement duties at the same time as it attempts to establish or re-establish local police capacity and train local police to assume responsibility for the provision of law and order. Policing in Kosovo and East Timor, therefore, is qualitatively different from that of previous UN peace operations.

Thus far, there has been relatively little substantive consideration of the significance of the international community's assumption of responsibility for policing. The immediate consequences of Kosovo and East Timor for international policing were certainly recognized and received significant media and political attention on various occasions during 1999–2000. The focus, however, was on the shortage of international police personnel for the operations. Attention centred on ways and means of increasing the number of police personnel contributed to the missions and accelerating deployment once a commitment was made.[6] Much less attention was given to what those police should do once they arrived in Kosovo or East Timor and how these policing operations were to be conceived and executed.[7] This book sets out to fill this gap by looking at the concept and practice of executive policing itself. The challenges of executive policing and its implications for international peace operations—political, legal, financial and administrative—are the questions it seeks to address.

II. Why executive policing?

It is useful to examine why executive policing was made part of two peace operations in the second half of 1999. There are numerous examples around the world of societies facing similar problems to Kosovo and East Timor, and UN peace operations were launched at around the same time in the Democratic Republic of the Congo (DRC) and Sierra Leone. Yet only in Kosovo and East Timor did the UN Security Council decide to assume transitional authority and responsibility for law and order. (There are, of course, differences between the origins of the two, but this book does not explore them.)

[6] See, e.g., Buchan, D., 'Peacekeepers arrest 46 after Kosovo clash', *Financial Times*, 15 Feb. 2000, p. 2; and Fitchett, J., 'In a cop-out, Europeans fail to supply promised police', *International Herald Tribune*, 22 Feb. 2000.

[7] Increasing attention is being paid to police in peace operations. See in particular Hansen, A. S., International Institute for Strategic Studies, *From Congo to Kosovo: Civilian Police in Peace Operations*, Adelphi Paper no. 343 (Oxford University Press: London, 2002); and Hills, A., 'The inherent limits of military forces in police peace operations', *International Peacekeeping*, vol. 8, no. 3 (autumn 2001), pp. 79–98.

In the case of Kosovo the need for the NATO member states to justify and demonstrate the success of their intervention in Kosovo, the political interest of the USA and Europeans in stabilizing the Balkans, and the desire of the UN to reassert its position in international peace operations all contributed to a 'maximal concept' of the peace operation. In the case of East Timor, three factors worked to encourage a general demand for the UN to assume authority: (*a*) the sense of UN and international failure in not having acted to prevent the predictable explosion of conflict that followed the East Timorese referendum on independence in August 1999; (*b*) the increasingly apparent weakness of Indonesia, the occupying power; and (*c*) the overwhelming desire of the East Timorese for independent statehood. Both Kosovo and East Timor received intense media coverage around the world and elicited strong public reactions, further influencing policy makers. In both cases, apparent international willingness to commit significant political, personnel and financial resources to rehabilitation and reconstruction made executive policing conceivable. The relatively small territorial and population size of both territories appeared to make it feasible.

Crucial though these factors were, the immediate factors behind the establishment of the two operations do not entirely explain why executive policing was a central element of both. The longer-term conditions which led the UN to assume responsibility for law enforcement in both were changes in the international political system, the evolving nature of peace operations and the gradual expansion of international policing tasks in them. These factors are also important in assessing the objectives of international policy makers and the extent to which these goals are achievable.

First, the trend in international politics away from the notion that the principle of state sovereignty is sacrosanct has produced a context in which the idea of executive policing is no longer inconceivable. The NATO intervention in Kosovo and the subsequent establishment of the UN transitional administration in the province highlighted this issue and fuelled the debate on the legitimacy of international intervention. UN Secretary-General Kofi Annan articulated the emerging view of the conditionality of sovereignty in the face of the primacy of individual human rights in September 1999, arguing that the state is an instrument of its people and that state sovereignty must be understood in relation to its people.[8] A year later Annan spelled out the implications of this: 'In circumstances in which universally accepted human rights are being violated on a massive scale we have a responsibility to act'.[9] Although the debate on intervention in Kosovo illustrated that Annan's view may not be universally shared, the widespread support among UN member states for the establishment of transitional authorities in both Kosovo and East Timor reflects a growing recognition that internal law and order are no longer the exclusive concern of the sovereign state.[10] As a consequence, the instruments and methods used by the state to provide and maintain law and order become a legitimate subject of international attention and assessment.

A second, related trend, facilitated by the end of the cold war superpower rivalry, has been the increased attention paid to the causes of conflict and, in particular, intra-state conflict. At the UN Millennium Summit in September 2000 the Security Council formally acknowledged economic, social, cultural and humanitarian grievances as root causes of armed conflict.[11] This declaration reflected a much wider debate on the link between governance, development and conflict, and the growing sense of many in the international aid community that the democratic and transparent rule of law is an essential component of stable development. International assistance, in this perspective, must address the way internal order is regulated within a state and how its citizens are governed. Moreover, it must be comprehensive and structurally focused if it is to lay the foundations for long-term, sustainable peace. States such as Canada, Norway, Sweden and the UK emphasize security sector reform within their national development aid programmes while the World Bank and the Organisation for Economic Co-operation and Development (OECD) have identified it as a priority issue.[12]

---

[8] Annan, K., 'Two concepts of sovereignty', *The Economist*, 18 Sep. 1999, pp. 49–50.

[9] United Nations, Report of the Secretary-General of the work of the organization, UN document A/55/1, 30 Aug. 2000.

[10] See, e.g., International Commission on Intervention and State Sovereignty, *The Responsibility to Protect* (International Development Research Centre: Ottawa, Dec. 2001).

[11] UN Security Council Resolution 1318, 7 Sep. 2000.

[12] The greater public attention being paid to international police reform efforts is one consequence of this. See, e.g., Organisation for Economic Co-operation and Development (OECD), Development Assistance Committee, Task Force on Conflict, Peace and Development Cooperation, 'Security sector reform as a development issue', Paris, 2–3 June 1999; Ball, N., 'Spreading good practices in security sector reform: policy options for the British Government', Overseas Development Council, Washington, DC, Nov. 1998; and Chanaa, J.,

Kosovo and East Timor were clear examples of conflict emerging from sustained repression and abuse of human rights. Comprehensive international engagement in internal law and order was perceived as vital in both cases—in the case of East Timor to help it establish sustainable independent statehood, and in the case of Kosovo to replace state repression and lay the foundations for provincial autonomy within a rehabilitated FRY.

A third factor shaping the environment from which executive policing emerged in 1999 was the experience of international policing in peace operations over the past decade. In many situations civilian police were already pushing at the boundaries of the SMART concept and blurring the distinction between monitoring and performing law enforcement. A clear example of this was the UN Transitional Administration in Cambodia (UNTAC) in 1992–95. Although the UN was given substantial authority to supervise the implementation of the Cambodian peace settlement, the assumption was that it would carry out its tasks on the basis of consensus from the local parties. The international CivPol presence therefore did not assume responsibility for the maintenance of law and order. As the transition got under way, however, and preparations for national elections began, local police officials displayed little willingness to curb growing political violence or investigate abuses of human rights. UNTAC, and its 3600-strong CivPol component, took on increasing responsibility for providing security in the Cambodian elections, guarding polling stations and preventing the harassment of voters.[13] The failure of the Cambodian judiciary to investigate human rights abuses led UNTAC to set up a Special UN Prosecutor under whom the UNTAC Police had the authority to arrest and detain suspects for charge.

Similar gaps in local law enforcement capacity led the international presences in Haiti and Somalia to take on a law and order capacity. The US-led Multi-national Force (MNF) which intervened in Haiti in 1994 was sanctioned by the UN, which provided international police monitors (IPMs) to the force until it was replaced by a UN operation, the UN Mission in Haiti (UNMIH). IPMs and subsequent UNMIH civilian police were authorized to enforce Haitian law when no local

International Institute for Strategic Studies, *Security Sector Reform: Issues, Challenges and Prospects*, Adelphi Paper no. 344 (Oxford University Press: London, 2002).

[13] Doyle M., 'Authority and elections in Cambodia', eds M. Doyle, I. Johnstone and R. Orr, *Keeping the Peace: Multidimensional UN Operations in Cambodia and El Salvador* (Cambridge University Press: Cambridge, 1997).

security forces were present and to intervene to prevent loss of life or disruption of a 'safe and secure' environment. They were also armed.[14] International police carried out these responsibilities until a new Haitian national police force was trained and in place. The ineffectiveness of the state policing structures in Somalia in 1992 led the US-led United Task Force (UNITAF) to establish an interim Auxiliary Security Force (ASF) to enforce locally agreed laws. Although Somalis made up the force, international military police provided support to the ASF in carrying out policing tasks.[15]

Closer to Kosovo, the UN Transitional Administration in Eastern Slavonia (UNTAES) and the nearby UN Mission in Bosnia and Herzegovina (UNMIBH) had seen the international police presence take on significant responsibility for supervising the reform of local police forces, including capacity to investigate and take disciplinary action against local police officers.[16] The head of UNTAES had managerial and operational control over the newly-established temporary police force, while UNMIBH has the authority to vet and certify all Bosnian police officers.

International police involvement in maintaining law and order in all these cases was limited and piecemeal, and was usually in response to events on the ground—a chaotic internal security environment (e.g., in Somalia), the absence or complete rejection of local police forces (e.g., in Haiti), or the unwillingness of local law enforcement officials to cooperate and pursue agreed reforms (e.g., in Bosnia and Cambodia). Moreover, it was usually unsatisfactory. The involvement of international personnel in particular instances did little to contribute to the overall reform of law and order in the countries concerned. It was often fruitless, especially in cases of the investigation and arrest of persons suspected of human rights abuses, given the lack of accompanying judicial and penal reform. Only in the case of UNTAES, where the international presence was backed by wide-ranging powers, did the assumption of partial policing powers achieve lasting results.

---

[14] Bailey M. *et al.*, 'Haiti: military–police partnership for public security', eds R. B. Oakley, M. J. Dziedzic and E. M. Goldberg, *Policing the New World Disorder: Peace Operations and Public Security* (National Defence University Press: Washington, DC, 1998), pp. 215–52.

[15] The only state participating in UNITAF which contributed civilian police to the mission was Australia.

[16] Holm, T. T., 'CivPol operations in Eastern Slavonia, 1992–98', *International Peacekeeping*, vol. 6, no. 4 (winter 1999), p. 148.

The lack of success in such instances prompted some police experts to point to the danger of 'expansive' policing in peace operations. Yet a return to strict monitoring and training-only operations offered little attraction. The examples of El Salvador and Guatemala illustrate the difficulty of bringing about comprehensive, sustainable police reform in a context where the international police presence has little power other than to cajole and convince authorities and police officers of the need for change.[17] The SMART concept of international policing came up against the sheer scale of the disorder in post-conflict environments and the sheer complexity of sustainable peace-building. As the most comprehensive review of UN peace operations, the Brahimi Report, noted one year after the start of UNMIK: 'The modern role of civilian police needs to be better understood and developed. In short, a doctrinal shift is required in how the Organisation conceives of and utilises civilian police in peace operations'.[18]

The logic, for some, was clear: to effect lasting change to law and order in the context of a divided, post-conflict society, the authority to put in place and supervise a comprehensive framework for law and order was a prerequisite. Kosovo and East Timor provided perfect test cases for such models to be established.

III. Executive policing in this book

Executive policing in Kosovo and East Timor represents a break with the past but has a substantial background of international policing in the past. The six authors in this book explore this conundrum, focusing on the design and implementation of executive policing in both cases and, in so doing, raising practical and conceptual issues involved in executive policing. In looking at different aspects of international law enforcement in Kosovo and East Timor, they help to construct a framework within which the concept and practice of executive policing can be examined and preliminary observations made.

Colette Rausch explores the means by which international police legitimately assumed responsibility for law enforcement in Kosovo and East Timor, and the legal framework in which executive policing

---

[17] Stanley, W., 'Building new police forces in El Salvador and Guatemala: learning and counter-learning', *International Peacekeeping*, vol. 6, no. 4 (1999), pp. 113–34.

[18] United Nations, Report of the Panel on United Nations Peace Operations, UN document A/55/305, S/2000/809, 21 Aug. 2000 (the Brahimi Report).

takes place. She draws attention to the practical difficulties involved in policing where the applicable law is unknown or uncertain.

Two writers look at the types of policing involved in law enforcement in peace operations. Michael J. Dziedzic focuses on Kosovo and looks at the challenges international actors face in designing a strategy for law enforcement in a post-conflict environment. In this context, policing and peace implementation are intertwined: Dziedzic explores how this relationship shapes law enforcement by the police component of a peace operation. Eirin Mobekk's contribution concentrates on East Timor and the attempt by the international police element there to introduce community policing into its practice of law enforcement. She examines the difficulties foreign police face in trying to implement civil society-focused models of policing in an unfamiliar environment.

The pivotal relationship between the military and police elements of a peace operation is discussed by Annika S. Hansen. The relationship takes on special significance in an executive policing operation, where military peacekeepers provide the coercive underpinnings for the international law enforcement effort. She argues that there are structural and practical impediments to successful cooperation between the international military and police, and discusses how the divisions of labour established between them in Kosovo and East Timor have attempted to tackle such challenges.

The final two chapters of the book focus on the basis for ending executive police operations. The question of local police training is central to almost every international police operation, not least as it is the key to terminating the international police presence. Robert Perito looks at the particular demands where training of local police is part of an executive policing operation and has to be balanced against law enforcement duties. Eric Scheye addresses a question that is belatedly receiving attention, namely, the structural and institutional efforts required to build a sustainable law enforcement system in a country. International police operations have, according to Scheye, been slow to take on board this fundamental element of rule-of-law reform. Executive policing, however, makes it impossible to ignore the institutional development of local police forces, and Scheye looks at some of the ways in which this can be done. The book concludes with a short chapter highlighting some of the central themes raised by the six authors, all of which raise further questions for continued research.

2. The assumption of authority in Kosovo and East Timor: legal and practical implications

*Colette Rausch**

I. Introduction

This chapter gives an overview of the instruments and documents that comprise the legal framework for the police components in the United Nations missions in Kosovo and East Timor. The legal framework is particularly important given the broad law-enforcement powers of the international police in these missions. These powers include carrying arms, making investigations, arrest and detention. The chapter then discusses in more detail the practical issues related to enforcing the law in a post-conflict environment.

The legal framework for executive policing comprises a number of instruments, including: (*a*) the UN Security Council resolutions which establish and provide authority to the missions; (*b*) other United Nations resolutions, rules and regulations, standard operating procedures, policies and guidelines; and (*c*) the laws deemed by the UN to be applicable in the mission. The task of interpreting and implementing these instruments in the day-to-day activity of the international police operating in executive missions is daunting given the complex issues and challenges that face them.

The UN took action in both Kosovo and East Timor on the basis of the authority of the Security Council under Chapter VII of the UN Charter. Such authority is based on Article 39 when the Security Council finds that there exists a 'threat to the peace, breach of the peace or act of aggression'. The mandates vested all legislative and executive authority, including the administration of justice, in the two UN administrations. It is this authority that is read as giving international police in Kosovo and East Timor the right to carry weapons and engage in fully fledged law enforcement duties.

* The author would like to thank all the former and present international police officers, members of the UN missions in Kosovo and East Timor, and others who generously shared their expertise in the preparation of this chapter.

UN Security Council Resolution 1244 established the UN Interim Administration Mission in Kosovo (UNMIK).[1] It states that UNMIK will provide a 'transitional administration for the people of Kosovo' and 'oversee the development of provisional democratic and self-governing institutions to ensure conditions for a peaceful and normal life for all inhabitants of Kosovo'. Although all the elements of UNMIK's mandate relate to some degree to the international police component, two in particular concern it more directly. These are the elements which give UNMIK the responsibility of 'maintaining civil law and order, including establishing local police forces and meanwhile through the deployment of international police personnel to serve in Kosovo' and by 'protecting and promoting human rights'.[2]

UN Security Council Resolution 1272 established the UN Transitional Administration in East Timor (UNTAET).[3] It gave UNTAET overall responsibility for the administration of East Timor and empowered it to exercise all legislative and executive authority, including the administration of justice. Particularly relevant to the international police are the clauses that give UNTAET the responsibility to 'provide security and maintain law and order throughout the territory of East Timor'.[4]

The mandates themselves provide no substantive guidance to the international police as to how to carry out their duties. They simply tell them to maintain law and order. International police must therefore look to other documents in addition to the mandates. The international police in Kosovo and East Timor are governed, for example, by the Code of Conduct for Law Enforcement Officials[5] and the UN Basic Principles on the Use of Force and Firearms by Law Enforce-

---

[1] UN Security Council Resolution 1244, 10 June 1999, reproduced in appendix A in this volume. See also UNMIK Regulation 1999/1, 25 July 1999, para. 1.1: 'All legislative and executive authority with respect to Kosovo, including the administration of the judiciary, is vested in UNMIK and is exercised by the Special Representative of the Secretary General'. All UNMIK regulations are available on the UNMIK Internet site at URL <http://www.un.org/peace/kosovo/pages/regulations/regs.html>.

[2] UN Security Council Resolution 1244 (note 1), paras 11(i) and (j).

[3] UN Security Council Resolution 1272, 25 Oct. 1999, reproduced in appendix A. in this volume See also UNTAET Regulation 1999/1, 27 Nov. 1999, para. 1.1: 'All legislative and executive authority with respect to East Timor, including the administration of the judiciary, is vested in UNTAET and is exercised by the Transitional Administrator'. All UNTAET regulations are available on the UNTAET Internet site at URL <http://www.un.org/peace/etimor/UntaetN.htm>.

[4] UN Security Council Resolution 1272 (note 3), para. 2(a).

[5] UN General Assembly Resolution 34/16, 17 Dec. 1979.

ment Officials.[6] Both these instruments set out the rules regarding the use of force by civilian police. According to the latter, force may only be used when absolutely necessary and then only to the extent required to perform legitimate law-enforcement functions.

The UN has also published a handbook, *United Nations Civilian Police Principles and Guidelines*.[7] According to the preface, the handbook does not 'replace or supersede the Rules and Regulations of the UN, related administrative issuances or Standard Operating Procedures of peacekeeping field operations, or other United Nations directives'. Its purpose is to assist member states which contribute police in preparing them for deployment and help UN senior management who are tasked with planning and operational duties. The UN has also published a guide called the 'UN Blue Book' which summarizes the international standards and norms involving basic principles of criminal justice, human rights and humanitarian law for the use of the civilian police components of UN peacekeeping operations.[8] Although not legally binding, the handbooks provide substantive guidance. In addition, there are a number of standards that must be developed within a mission to dictate how the police must operate— on the use of force, arrest and detention, and the use, storage, carrying and maintenance of weapons. UNMIK and UNTAET have both developed policies governing these areas.[9] These standards are legally binding on the international police.

II. Applicable law and 'legal anarchy'

It is of critical importance that all civilian police are seen to be applying the law equitably and consistently. Before engaging in their policing functions, in addition to understanding the political environment and cultural norms, the international police must be thoroughly

[6] Eighth United Nations Congress on the Prevention of Crime and the Treatment of Offenders, welcomed by General Assembly Resolution 45/121, 18 Dec. 1990.

[7] United Nations, Department of Peace-keeping Operations, *United Nations Civilian Police Principles and Guidelines* (UN: New York, 2001) sets out the DPKO's and Civilian Police Unit's policies on international police operations.

[8] The UN Blue Book is available at URL <http://www.uncjin.org/Documents/ BlueBook/BlueBook/>. The topics covered include the role of the police, arrest, force and firearms, trials, victims, detainees and prisoners, torture and other cruel treatment, illegal executions, genocide, humanitarian rules and refugee protection.

[9] UN Mission in Kosovo, 'UNMIK standard operating procedures' (undated); and UN Transitional Administration in East Timor, 'UNTAET CIVPOL administration and operations manual' (undated) and 'UNTAET rules of engagement for the Police Component' (undated).

briefed about and become familiar with all the laws they will be enforcing and the judicial system in which they will be working. The first thing they need to know when they arrive is: What is the law that is to be enforced? What are the criminal provisions that I will need to apply in my duties? What is my role in relation to the prosecutor and judge? What is my role in relation to the military peacekeeping forces? In Kosovo and East Timor, when the international police arrived, these questions were not easily answered. Even once it was decided what laws applied, interpretations and applications of the laws differed between the legal actors on the scene.

Choosing the law to be applied

Upon the UN administration's arrival in both Kosovo and East Timor, it was decided that the applicable law in each territory would be the laws that had applied prior to the adoption of the mandate of each mission insofar as they were consistent with internationally recognized human rights standards, the mandate of each mission and any subsequently promulgated regulation.[10] This seemed at the time to be a reasonable way to approach the issue to ensure that a legal vacuum did not occur and that the applicable law would be familiar to those it would govern. Further, it was believed that applying the prior law in Kosovo would be consistent with the commitment in Security Council Resolution 1244 to maintaining the sovereignty and territorial integrity of the Federal Republic of Yugoslavia (FRY).[11] In East Timor, the decision meant that the applicable law would be derived from Indonesian law. The East Timorese did not reject this decision. In Kosovo, however, this was not the case. The Kosovars viewed the applicable law decision as validating Serbian law, which they found oppressive and therefore unacceptable.

The applicable law in Kosovo was initially established by regulation in July 1999.[12] To summarize, this first regulation stated that the applicable law was to be the laws that were in effect in Kosovo on 24 March 1999 insofar as they did not conflict with internationally recognized human rights standards, regulations adopted by UNMIK or the fulfilment of the mandate under Resolution 1244.

[10] UNMIK Regulation 1999/1 (note 1); and UNTAET Regulation 1999/1 (note 3).
[11] UN Security Council Resolution 1244 provides that Kosovo shall have substantial autonomy within the FRY.
[12] UNMIK Regulation 1999/1 (note 1).

This regulation faced political opposition from the Kosovar Albanian legal community, who argued that the laws in effect on 24 March 1999 discriminated against non-Serbs and were used as a tool of oppression by the Serbian authorities, and that the Serbian authorities' revocation of Kosovo's autonomy in 1989 violated the constitution of the FRY. From the Kosovar Albanians' perspective, therefore, the Kosovo Code and the laws in effect in 1989 were still applicable. The UN had not anticipated this backlash.

The UN lawyers argued that any provisions in any of the former laws that were discriminatory would not be applied. However, they were not successful in convincing the Kosovar Albanian legal community.[13] Eventually, in December 1999, the UN acquiesced and adopted a second regulation on the applicable law.[14] Section 1.1 of this new regulation provided that the applicable law was the law in effect in Kosovo on 22 March 1989 and all UNMIK regulations promulgated. If the prior laws and the regulations conflicted, the regulations would take precedence. Section 1.3 of the new regulation provided that internationally recognized human rights standards would be applied and set out a list of eight human rights instruments. It further provided that if a 'subject matter or situation is not covered by the laws set out in section 1 of the present regulation but is covered by another law in force in Kosovo after 22 March 1989 which is not discriminatory and which complies with section 3 of the present regulation, the court, body or person shall, as an exception, apply that law'. The end result was that the FRY Criminal Procedure Code, the Serbian Criminal Code, the Yugoslav Criminal Code and the Kosovo Criminal Code were applicable to criminal matters in Kosovo.

Problems in implementing the applicable law

Although the political dispute as to the question of the law applicable in Kosovo was resolved, the practical issues remained. The new regu-

---

[13] The Kosovar Albanians' arguments were based not solely on the content of the laws themselves but primarily on political underpinnings involving the loss of their autonomy, and on the unfair application of the laws against them in the past by the Serb authorities. In their content, the 1989 laws were not very different from the 1999 laws, except that some of the codes contained provisions that the others did not. For example, the Serbian Criminal Code contained a provision on kidnapping, whereas the Kosovo Criminal Code did not. The Yugoslav Criminal Code contained a provision on war crimes, whereas the Kosovo Criminal Code and Serbian Criminal Code did not.

[14] 'On the law applicable in Kosovo', UNMIK Regulation 1999/24, 12 Dec. 1999.

lation merely created more confusion regarding the applicable law as disputes arose over the interpretation of certain provisions in the new regulation. In addition, regulations adopted by UNMIK were not always drafted or conceived in such a way as to be consistent with local laws. Local and international experts were not always consulted. Even when local experts were consulted and provided meaningful comments, their comments were not always incorporated. Some of the criminal provisions were not consistent with the civil law system of Kosovo and some international human rights experts argued that they were not consistent with the European Convention on Human Rights. Local judges and prosecutors thus did not always interpret them in the same way or understand them in the same way as police officers from other legal systems. This was especially true with police from common law countries.[15] Such disparity affected the outcome of cases.[16]

The new regulation allowed the police and judiciary to pick and choose the laws they wished to apply. The result was that the Kosovar Albanian judges were applying the law that they found to be legitimate—the law in effect in 1989—while Serbian judges continued to apply the law that was in effect in 1999. Moreover, the 'applicable law' was changed in mid-stream and individuals were prosecuted under different 'applicable laws' depending on when they were arrested. This is arguably contrary to the principle of legal certainty. In an environment like that of Kosovo, where international judges and prosecutors were appointed because of allegations that members of the local judiciary were ethnically biased and were subjected to threats and pressure in politically motivated cases, vagueness in the provisions and lack of legal certainly exacerbate these problems.[17]

---

[15] E.g., under the applicable law, a written notice of arrest must be provided to each person arrested if he or she is held for 24 hours or more. According to an international judge, international police frequently fail to comply with this requirement. Instead, they simply complete a police report for the file and in some cases also verbally notify the arrestee as to why he or she is being arrested. Neither procedure complies with the applicable law. The written notice of arrest is important in that it triggers the timeline for appeal.

[16] E.g., according to an international prosecutor, during a house search, military police found hand grenades and an AK-47 assault rifle under a bed. When questioned, the family members present told the military police that it was the room of their 2 brothers. The military police did no further investigation (e.g., collecting evidence in the room, such as pictures, telephone records or ID cards showing who was living there) to determine who had control of the room, but the statements of the family members could not be used because under applicable law they were considered 'privileged' witnesses and could not be called as witnesses. In the end it was not possible to prosecute the case because of lack of evidence.

[17] E.g., according to an international prosecutor, a Kosovar Serb was arrested and under investigation for violation of a Yugoslav Criminal Code provision following allegations that he had slashed the tyres of an UNMIK vehicle. The Kosovar Albanian judiciary detained him

Even once it was made clear by regulation which body of law was to be applied, the laws in Kosovo were not readily available in Albanian, Serbian and English. It was not until months later that international organizations got together, made a compilation of the laws in all three languages and made it available to the local judiciary and those in the international community charged with the administration of justice, including the international police.[18] However, distribution was on an ad hoc basis and was not widespread, and the compilations included only the actual laws themselves with no available commentary. In some cases, the English translation was not accurate or had missing provisions or words. In other cases it was not always clear, and where it was clear the provisions contained terms and concepts that were foreign to someone new to the Kosovo legal system.

No clear guidelines existed to guide the police in the procedures for making arrests, gathering evidence or detaining suspects. To make matters more difficult, the international police did not apply either the Kosovar or the Serbian law at all times. In the light of the confusion as to which law applied and the difficulty of understanding the provisions, many resorted to applying the law as they knew it from their own systems. Generally speaking, this practice may not pose widespread problems as most criminal codes contain provisions for common crimes. However, there are exceptions. For example, in Kosovo possession of drugs is not listed as a crime in the criminal codes, but international police who come from countries which do criminalize possession often arrest suspects for possession of drugs. Furthermore, not every country that provides civilian police officers has laws that necessarily comport with international human rights standards. Matters such as arrest, interrogation, detention and searches are sensitive areas and civilian police officers simply applying the law from home may well run foul of international human rights standards.

for just over 1 year. However, when a Kosovar Albanian was arrested and under investigation for a property offence of the same gravity against UNMIK, the same judiciary used a Kosovo Criminal Code provision that was less onerous than the Yugoslav Criminal Code provision and the suspect was not detained. UNMIK Regulation 2000/64, 'On assignment of international judges/prosecutors and/or change of venue', 15 Dec. 2000, allows for the appointment of international judges and prosecutors and/or a change of venue 'where this is considered necessary to ensure the independence and impartiality of the judiciary or the proper administration of justice'.

[18] The American Bar Association Central and East European Law Initiative (ABA/CEELI) started the initiative and compiled criminal-related laws. They then worked together with the Organization for Security and Co-operation in Europe (OSCE) and the Kosovo Law Centre to publish the compilation.

The criminal procedure codes that govern matters of arrest, search, investigation and detention vary from system to system, and mis-application can result directly in the loss of evidence or of a case.[19]

In East Timor, limited numbers of copies of the Indonesian laws were available. Only parts of the laws were in English. Translation took a long time. International standards instruments were not distributed. As in Kosovo, access to the laws was lacking in East Timor.

In both Kosovo and East Timor, all these issues made teaching and mentoring of local police difficult: the international police who were to teach the law did not know the law themselves. Those international police officers with initiative who made great efforts to track down the law and consult knowledgeable persons were able to get copies of and begin to understand the applicable law, but this is a daunting task on top of day-to-day duties, especially considering the fact that the applicable law is new to the international police officer and new laws are being promulgated along the way.

In Kosovo, international lawyers debated the interpretation of the regulation and how to apply it. Furthermore, they frequently discussed and continue to discuss how to apply the human rights instruments to the criminal provisions. How do the instruments and the provisions work together? Can someone be detained for 24, 48 or 72 hours or longer before being taken before a judge? What are the rules for questioning of witnesses or suspects by police? Can the detainee have access to defence counsel? At what stage? All these uncertainties disputed among international lawyers combined with much theoretical and academic debate did little to help the police officer on the street who just wanted practical and straightforward guidance.

Furthermore, there was sometimes a disparity between what human rights experts in the field argued was required under international human rights standards and what police argued was actually possible to do given the circumstances in the field. What was missing, and critical to effective law enforcement and adherence to international human rights standards, was a meaningful dialogue between experienced lawyers with human rights experience and criminal justice

---

[19] E.g., as a matter of routine, the international police in Kosovo would take statements from accused persons. This is standard practice in many countries. However, under the FRY Criminal Procedure Code these statements cannot be used against the accused at his or her trial. To be used in court, a statement from the accused must be taken at the direction of the investigating judge. International police were dismayed to learn that an accused person when testifying in court could say something completely different from what he or she had said in his or her statement to the police and no reference could be made to that statement.

experience, the international police (and later the international judges and prosecutors who came on board), the military, local judges, prosecutors and police, and legal experts. These actors needed to come together and discuss, from both a practical and a legal standpoint, what could be done that would be consistent with international human rights standards and still be feasible given the reality in the field.

Instead, there were institutional battles and the 'human rights' component became polarized from the 'law enforcement' component. In fact these two concepts are not mutually exclusive: the interests can be balanced when experienced and constructive people who know the subject matter and the reality in the field work together.

For roughly the first year of the mission in Kosovo the international police carried out their duties on the basis of whatever assumptions they could make about what the laws were, what they might have heard from the local judges or prosecutors with whom they were working or, more often, their own understanding of law from their own countries. This resulted in some police actions that violated the applicable law.[20] In the second year of the mission operational bulletins and guidelines were slowly developed to help police determine how long they could hold a suspect before taking him or her before a judge, how to make an incident report, how to execute a search warrant, and the procedures for arrest and detention.

Efforts were made to prepare a field manual for the international police in Kosovo that would be both user-friendly and in a form that could be taken to the field. Under the auspices of the Organization for Security and Co-operation in Europe (OSCE), a team of police, lawyers and experts prepared a comprehensive draft that was ready in the summer of 2000. It was held up by institutional battles and has yet to be published. The UN Department of Judicial Affairs put together a shorter field manual in September 2000.[21] However, international police did not find this manual to be of substantive help. Although it did provide explanations relating to the role of the police, the investigating judge and the court as set out in the applicable criminal procedure code, it did not provide the needed guidance in the critical areas of arrest, detention and access to counsel.

In East Timor, UN lawyers who had provided guidance in the initial stages of the Kosovo mission also contributed, and had the lessons of

---

[20] See note 19.

[21] This was in the form of a photocopied set of pages distributed at training sessions.

Kosovo to assist them. Through a regulation entitled the Transitional Rules of Criminal Procedure,[22] the administration in East Timor tried to provide clear and consistent procedures to guide the international police in areas such as arrest, detention and detainee access to defence counsel. This meant that the international police were required to follow the Indonesian Penal Code, the Indonesian Criminal Procedure Code and the Transitional Rules of Criminal Procedure. Unfortunately, these rules created confusion among the international police. Some used the Transitional Rules. Others referred to all three parts of the law. As in Kosovo, all complained that they were not properly trained in any of the laws prior to having to enforce them. Also as in Kosovo, when they could not be certain of the law, they resorted by and large to trying to be fair and applying the laws they knew from home. Police from civil law, common law and Islamic legal systems and even countries where customary or tribal law applies were performing day-to-day policing and observing different standards. The result was that Kosovars and East Timorese were subjected to different applications of the law depending on who the police officer was and what system he or she came from. The quality and effect of police work differed from district to district and from officer to officer.

In addition, in Kosovo, the police were 'grafted' onto a system with a socialist heritage where independence of the judiciary did not exist and the relationship between the police, the prosecutor and the judge was quite different from the relationship in many of the countries that supplied international police.

It could have helped both missions if model codes and procedures had been available at the outset of the missions. In the Brahimi Report mention was made of the absence of clarity about the applicable law which plagued the peacekeeping operations in Kosovo and East Timor. The report recommended a 'model code' that could be used in peacekeeping operations. According to the report, '[t]hese missions' tasks would have been much easier if a common United Nations justice package had allowed them to apply an interim legal code to which mission personnel could have been pre-trained while the final answer to the "applicable law" question was being worked out'.[23]

---

[22] UNTAET Regulation 2000/30, 25 Sep. 2000, as amended by UNTAET Regulation 2001/25, 14 Sep. 2001.

[23] United Nations, Report of the Panel on United Nations Peace Operations, UN document A/55/305, S/2000/809, 21 Aug. 2000 (the Brahimi Report), paras 79–80. Together with the Irish Human Rights Centre, experts from the UN, and practitioners from the military, police,

Determining the applicable law is a challenge for an incoming peacekeeping operation when a measure of legal code reform is needed in any case to bring a pre-existing law into line with international human rights standards. In the meantime, arrests take place and, in the case of executive missions, new laws continue to be promulgated,[24] thus creating more confusion.

A stand-by emergency criminal code and criminal procedure code, including police laws, which can be adapted for use immediately upon the arrival of international peacekeeping personnel, are needed. The stand-by code provisions should be detailed enough to provide guidance to police officers, military personnel, lawyers, judges and defence lawyers. They should spell out the precise parameters, such as time limits and requirements for arrest, detention and searches, and incorporate provisions and standards that are widely accepted in different legal systems. They would also need to take into account the fact that the needs and legal traditions of individual countries differ. To have a lawful society, the law must be viewed as legitimate by the society. There are often legal traditions in a country that may be contrary to international human rights standards but are fully part of the country's culture and legal practice, and therefore viewed as legitimate. Annotations or alternatives could help here. After the emergency phase, the interim legal codes could be the core of the larger reform process when there is time to consider the country's legal codes as a whole.

III. Engaging in law enforcement functions

Operating in a multi-country police force with rotating personnel

Even if the applicable law is clearly agreed upon from the outset, making sure that the international police from a multitude of countries with different legal systems are thoroughly versed and competent in the applicable law, the local justice system and effective investigative techniques for the local justice system is challenging, to say the least. In addition, police officers from different countries come with differ-

justice and humanitarian law sectors, the United States Institute of Peace (USIP) is developing such a 'package' of laws as part of its Peacekeeping and Administration of Justice Project. A description of the project can be found at URL <http://www.usip.org>.

[24] In Kosovo, the Special Representative of the Secretary-General (SRSG) has legislative authority to pass regulations and administrative directions that become part of the applicable law. In East Timor, the SRSG passes regulations that become part of the applicable law.

ing levels of English, firearms abilities, patrolling experience and investigative experience, and from different legal and cultural environments. In Kosovo the police came from approximately 53 countries. In East Timor, they came from 41 countries.

Furthermore, because of the nature of peacekeeping operations, most international police are on fairly short rotations. The average length is one year, only a minority of tours of duty are longer and they can be as short as six months. Too often, just when an international police officer settles down and becomes more competent in the job, he or she leaves, or just when a team comes together and begins to succeed as a team one or more of the members rotates out. This rotation of personnel and the varying backgrounds and levels of experience pose great challenges in putting together investigations, especially in more complex cases involving organized crime. The result, from a legal standpoint, is difficulty in maintaining coordination and continuity in long-term cases, especially those that require cultivating local informants.

Use of force is a critical issue. It is important above all that the UN principles are applied across the board.[25] Failure to do so results in unacceptable human rights violations and undermines the international community's efforts to show the public and the developing local police force that excessive force is unacceptable. In addition, criminal cases are lost and the UN may be subject to civil liability.[26] All cases of use of excessive force must be treated seriously and the perpetrators punished accordingly. Likewise, civilian police officers must be able to work in a multicultural environment and with both sexes. Not all police officers arrive with experience of or the willingness to work in such environments.

---

[25] According to a police officer who worked in Kosovo at the Kosovo Police School and an international prosecutor, the use of force and of warning shots became an issue. International police officers would apply different standards depending on where they came from. Where armed resistance is warranted, an officer operating under European standards will typically identify himself or herself as a police officer and tell the suspect to 'stop or I will shoot'. If the suspect does not stop, the police officer fires warning shots either in the air or at the ground. Sweden, e.g., teaches police officers to fire 2–3 shots in rapid succession. If the suspect still fails to stop, the police officer can then shoot to stop him, in the leg if the officer believes that this will stop him, or if not in the centre of the chest. Where to shoot is a decision made by the officer depending on the situation. US police officers do not fire warning shots. If a situation warrants it under the use-of-force continuum, they may shoot to stop and that means shooting in the centre of the chest. They do not shoot limbs. UNMIK Police procedures provide for the use of warning shots when deadly force is justified.

[26] E.g., in Kosovo the UN has paid compensation to individuals who had been unjustly detained in criminal cases.

Operating within the legal framework, available resources and cultural environment

In Kosovo the applicable law did not provide the tools needed to combat the types of crime international police face. Special investigative tools such as electronic surveillance, witness protection and the use of informants were non-existent. Police were not permitted by the UN to engage in controlled purchases of drugs or weapons. These inadequacies in the legal and resources framework make it difficult for the international police to investigate and pursue serious cases involving war crimes, organized crime, murder, violence against minorities, trafficking in women, kidnapping and so on. It was not until nearly 18 months into the peacekeeping operation that regulations were adopted to address some of these issues, and because of lack of resources and political will a comprehensive witness protection system is still not in place.

For administrative and budget reasons, international police do not always have the equipment they need to carry out successful investigations, for instance, telephone tapping. In East Timor the system suffered from the same lack of resources necessary to investigate and prosecute serious crimes.[27]

Lack of sufficient numbers of qualified personnel on both the police and the judicial side, local and international, makes it impossible to tackle these crimes adequately. The quality of the local judges and prosecutors varies. In Kosovo for some 10 years before the UN mission began, they had been 'kicked' from their positions by the Serb authorities. In some circumstances, some might have been able to continue working for a certain period of time, but they would have been considered traitors by their peers, so they did not. For this long period they were not engaged in judicial work and did not receive continuing training.

When the UN took over in East Timor, only a few East Timorese jurists existed and they had no experience as judges or prosecutors. The previous cadre of judges and prosecutors had fled East Timor with the Indonesian authorities. The judicial system struggled to function with young and inexperienced judges and prosecutors engaging in on-the-job training.

---

[27] Linton, S., 'Rising from the ashes: the creation of a viable criminal justice system in East Timor', *Melbourne University Law Review*, vol. 25 (2001).

In Kosovo international judges and prosecutors have been appointed to handle sensitive cases including war crimes, organized crime, and politically and ethnically motivated crimes. Unfortunately, the UN has been unable to recruit and retain sufficient numbers of qualified international judges and prosecutors. Some who were appointed did not have the legal experience or language skills necessary to handle the kinds of case they were expected to handle, and they do not always have the support they need from qualified translators and legal assistants. Police officers in East Timor also reported that there were not enough qualified interpreters to assist in their work.

Even if resources and adequate legal tools are in place, officers are faced with cultural challenges to doing their jobs. For example, more cases involving crimes such as rape and domestic violence are investigated and prosecuted in Western societies as law enforcement and the judiciary become more receptive and sensitive in pursuing cases and as victims become more willing to report crimes. This has not been the case in either Kosovo or East Timor. Furthermore, due to family relationships and fear of retaliation, it is often difficult to get the information needed for investigations. In Kosovo there is great hesitance to be an informant. Witnesses are reluctant to cooperate and a code of silence is often the norm.[28] Also, given the language and ethnic barriers, international police cannot simply 'go undercover' as they would in their own country.

In Kosovo it was possible from the outset of the mission to determine that ethnic-related crimes and organized crime would be prominent. Societies coming out of war are frequently faced with both types of crime, especially when a security vacuum exists, as was the case in Kosovo. Ethnically and politically motivated crimes and trafficking in women followed closely. It took well over a year before regulations were promulgated and mechanisms put into place to begin tackling these crimes, and then they were not adequate. Nor are they yet. Two-and-a-half years into the mission, the legal framework and adequate resources are still lacking.

This is a lesson for future missions. Proper attention needs to be given to the likely types of crime the peacekeepers will face. Then a

[28] This of course depends on the case. It is especially true in cases involving individuals who were part of the former Kosovo Liberation Army (KLA). Kosovar Albanians are reluctant to be seen as cooperating with law enforcement in cases that may be brought against these individuals, who are often seen as war heroes. However, they have not been hesitant about witnessing in cases against Serbs involving alleged war crimes.

strategy is required to address issues related to the legal framework, expertise and training needed to combat the particular types of crime.

In both Kosovo and East Timor, traditional or customary law existed, to varying degrees. In Kosovo its use grew strongly during the 10 years during which the province lost autonomy and the system of justice was run by the Serbian authorities. Viewing the Serbian-controlled police and judiciary as repressive, the Kosovar Albanians avoided the justice system and relied more and more on traditional methods of dispute resolution. This included resolving long-standing blood feuds by calling on a respected member of the community to act as mediator. In East Timor, the use of traditional means increased during the Indonesian occupation because, as in Kosovo, the local population did not trust the authorities. The traditional systems did not evaporate just because the UN had arrived in Kosovo and East Timor. Their use increases significantly once one moves away from Pristina or Dili and into villages and rural areas. This was especially true in cases involving domestic violence, marital disputes and even rape.

In Kosovo the use of traditional systems was never sanctioned by the UN, nor was there any attempt to have it incorporated somehow into the formal justice system. However, there were cases where international police, working with the newly deployed local police service, permitted its use in minor cases, such as traffic disputes. In East Timor it was discussed more openly and police officers in certain circumstances deferred to traditional mechanisms of dispute resolution, often because of lack of resources and perhaps also a desire to honour local custom. Senior officers in East Timor supported the use of the traditional system.[29] In the initial phase of the East Timor mission, the international police relied on the traditional system because there was no other system operating since the Indonesians had run the system before, and when they departed they took the judicial personnel with them.

Livestock trading was a traditional method of resolving disputes. According to an Australian international police officer, in one case, a teacher received a beating by people from one village who were upset by the way he taught. The teacher's village was angry about the assault. The international police allowed the dispute to be resolved between the village elders, who decided that the victim would receive

[29] Mobekk, E., 'Policing peace operations: United Nations civilian police in East Timor', Monograph for the John D. and Catherine T. MacArthur Foundation Program on Peace and International Co-operation, King's College, London, Oct. 2001.

a water buffalo and goats. In return, he would give a chicken to the other village. The two villages held a party afterwards and the situation was defused. In another case, a man touched a woman's breast. He was in fear of his life because the woman's village would make sure that he was banished from his village under pain of death. The matter was resolved by the man compensating the victim with a sincere expression of sorrow for what he had done together with a payment of goats and chickens, a traditional woven cloth and money. By turning to the traditional system of justice and quickly resolving these situations, the international police involved found that they were able to prevent things from getting out of control and assist in the healing process in the villages and among the victims.

Looking to traditional methods is not in itself a bad thing, but careful consideration is required as across-the-board acceptance may perpetuate inequities and violate international standards. The possible bias against women, children and minority ethnic groups in traditional mechanisms is problematic. There have been allegations of such injustices in both Kosovo and East Timor.[30] There are no guidelines in Kosovo or East Timor governing when the use of traditional methods is appropriate and when it is not. This just adds confusion and disparate treatment on top of the applicable law confusion.

Coordination and cooperation with the other components of the judicial system and the military

In Kosovo the international civilian police are under the control of UNMIK. The Kosovo Force (KFOR) is a military force and is separate from UNMIK with its own chain of command. In East Timor the international civilian police are under the control of UNTAET. The police and military are two separate, independent entities, and in post-conflict societies, where in the past the police and military were often combined to form an oppressive force, it is important that there is a clear separation of roles to foster community trust and acceptance of the civilian police force.

Because of the nature of peacekeeping operations, coordination and cooperation with the military are critical to effective executive pol-

---

[30] E.g., in a rape case in East Timor, the alleged perpetrator paid 9 water buffaloes to the victim's family in compensation. Mobekk (note 29), p. 34.

icing.[31] In Kosovo and East Timor, international civilian police have primacy in law enforcement matters, although in Kosovo the line has not always been so clear in practice. KFOR is sometimes involved in arrest and investigation functions. This has especially been the case where it finds itself involved by virtue of the security situation, for instance, in border and weapon cases during the Former Yugoslav Republic of Macedonia (FYROM) conflict in 2001, when fighters and those supporting them were crossing the Kosovo–FYROM border.

When the military is involved in such activities, coordination is required to ensure the proper transfer of evidence for cases originating with military and transferred to civilian authorities, so that information gathered through military intelligence means can be turned into evidence that can be used in court. In Kosovo important cases have been lost because of insufficient evidence that is admissible in court. Close coordination and care in the process of collecting evidence are needed in order to ensure that applicable law is taken into consideration. It is also important to ensure that investigations are not conducted at cross-purposes. In Kosovo military personnel raided brothels but were not coordinated with international police, who had ongoing investigations involving the same brothels. To prevent such incidents, both KFOR and the international police are striving to ensure cooperation, especially in the area of organized crime.

Coordination is critical in investigations involving war crimes, trafficking in women, political violence and the various crimes that come into the 'organized crime' category. The UNMIK Department of Justice (previously called the Department of Judicial Affairs) is creating a special unit where police, prosecutors and KFOR will work together to build cases using classified intelligence. The plan is for the military to provide support through intelligence that can be shared with prosecutors and/or investigators who have the necessary clearance. It is hoped that such intelligence can then lead to evidence that is admissible in court.

Equipment and logistics need to be shared because police generally do not have the equipment they need. In this regard, the military can greatly assist the civilian police. For example, when the International Force for East Timor (INTERFET) first landed in East Timor in September 1999, the Australian military police took on the job of finding the graves of those killed during the conflict and exhuming the

---

[31] See also chapter 5 in this volume.

bodies. They had the help of military doctors, video recording equipment and local Red Cross workers, and greatly assisted the international police assigned to conduct the investigations. The challenge was that there were no established guidelines for cooperation between the civilian authorities and the military, including the transfer of evidence and reporting forms. The result was confusion when the military handed over the cases to the civilian authorities.

Because of the way the Kosovo mission was set up,[32] much of the rule-of-law continuum—police, prosecution, judiciary and penal— was fragmented at the beginning. This posed operational problems which resulted in reduced levels of coordination and cooperation. It is of critical importance that the rule-of-law components work together in a continuum. The police and judicial bodies cannot work in parallel fashion. They must function as a unit—keeping in mind, of course, the principle of the independence of the judiciary. Eventually, UNMIK brought the police, prosecution, security and justice structures together under one administrative umbrella, the idea being that it would then have better coordination with other UNMIK structures and other organizations, including KFOR.

It is important to understand that the command and control structures, as well as the scope of the mandates, differ between the international police and the military. In both Kosovo and East Timor, international police found that the military, when called on to help, was not structured to respond as quickly as needed. Prior planning, communication and agreements can help reduce the gap. In any event, it is of the utmost importance that civilian police strive to understand the military's needs and goals, and vice versa. That way, both can go a fair way towards devising ways to work together.

---

[32] The international police were not fully deployed until over 2 months after the mission started. This gap left KFOR responsible for law enforcement activities. On the judicial side, initially, the decision was to let the judiciary be wholly local. The local judiciary was not fully mobilized until 8 months after the start of the mission. Many detainees were held for up to 6 months before there were enough judges to hold trials. Months later, international judges and prosecutors were brought in after a number of cases where ethnic bias against Serbs was demonstrated, as well as incidents of the judiciary apparently being influenced by former KLA members. On the penal side, initially no plans were made to address the need for detention and correctional facilities. During the gap period, KFOR was holding detainees, many in tents when buildings were not functional. Funding was almost non-existent. Penal experts were sent by certain countries and had to start from scratch.

IV. Accountability

It is essential that international police who commit crimes or are guilty of misconduct while on missions are subject to prosecution and/or disciplinary procedures, depending on the situation. Impunity is unacceptable given that international forces are always deployed to a situation where human rights have been violated and impunity is the norm. Establishing a system of rule of law begins with those who are deployed to do this. It is not acceptable for members of a local community to be held accountable for their actions while international actors are not. This disparity hampers efforts to establish the notion of equality before the law in a post-conflict society and weakens the credibility of the international police as a whole.

As discussed above, international police are subject to the mission's operating procedures in both Kosovo and East Timor. Allegations of offences are to be sent to the Office of Professional Standards in the UN, which investigates. Violations of the code can lead to disciplinary action. Civilian police may also be subject to the laws and disciplinary code of their home country if they are still serving police officers. The Convention on the Privileges and Immunities of the United Nations provides that UN officials and experts on missions for the UN are immune from personal arrest or detention,[33] but it also gives the UN Secretary-General the right to waive the immunity of any official or expert 'in any case where, in his opinion, the immunity would impede the course of justice and it can be waived without prejudice to the interest of the United Nations'.

In Kosovo, a parallel regulation was passed. Regulation 2000/47 provides that 'UNMIK personnel shall be immune from any form of arrest or detention'.[34] It further provides that the 'Secretary-General shall have the right and duty to waive the immunity of any UNMIK personnel in any case where, in his opinion, the immunity would impede the course of justice and can be waived without prejudice to the interest of UNMIK'.[35] The policy and procedure manual for the

---

[33] The Convention on the Privileges and Immunities of the United Nations was adopted by the UN General Assembly on 13 Feb. 1946 and entered into force on 17 Sep. 1946. It is available on the UN Internet site at URL <http://www.unog.ch/archives/un_priv.htm>.

[34] 'On the status, privileges and immunities of KFOR and UNMIK and their personnel in Kosovo', UNMIK Regulation 2000/47, 18 Aug. 2000, para. 3.4.

[35] UNMIK Regulation 2000/47 (note 34), para. 6.1. 'Personnel' are defined as 'United Nations officials, experts and other persons assigned to serve in any of the components of UNMIK and holding an ID card, which indicates that the holder is a member of UNMIK,

international police provides that UNMIK police officers 'have been granted immunity from personal arrest or detention for acts done while performing their official duties. The Secretary-General may, at his discretion, waive the UNMIK Police Officer's immunity'.[36] In East Timor the disciplinary code for international police contains a similar provision for immunity and waiver.[37]

Once immunity is waived, the international police may be prosecuted in the local courts for violations of applicable law. In Kosovo international police officers have been arrested and placed under judicial investigation for rape and murder.[38] However, an Austrian international police officer under investigation for beating and threatening to kill a man in police custody is alleged to have fled, with the assistance of his government, and returned to Austria. Austrian officials stated that he was repatriated for medical reasons only.[39] Human rights groups have alleged that countries often repatriate international police suspected of criminal conduct. Some international police believe that the worst thing that will happen to them if they engage in misconduct is that they will be sent home. The problem is further exacerbated by the frequent rotation of personnel. Even if action against an officer starts, that officer's term may well be over before the action is completed.

The issue of the accountability of international police must continue to receive attention, and structures must be enhanced to address the issue in a systematic and responsive fashion. The UN needs to have an articulated policy and set of guidelines to determine when waiver of immunity should be recommended. Each contributing nation must ensure that the international police it sends to missions are held accountable for misconduct and criminal activities. In cases of possible excessive use of force, in addition to police-led internal affairs investigations, thought should be given to having an independent body or panel conduct an additional investigation or exercise oversight.

issued by or under the authority of the Special Representative of the Secretary-General'. UNMIK Regulation 2000/47, sec. 1.

[36] 'UNMIK Police policy and procedure manual' (undated, unpublished), section 2, no. 2.10.4, p. 103.

[37] 'UNCIVPOL–UNTAET administration and operations manual, disciplinary code and procedure' (undated), section 1, no. 1.2, p. 23.

[38] E.g., an officer was arrested in Jan. 2002 after an ethnic Albanian woman was found shot in his flat. She later died in hospital.

[39] Lynch, C., 'Austria is said to aid flight of suspect: UN officials assail thwarting of probe', *Washington Post*, 6 Mar. 2002.

V. Conclusions

In Kosovo and East Timor, the military peacekeepers and international police entered environments where law and order vacuums existed and continued to exist to a degree that adversely affected efforts to create stability and systems based on the rule of law. In future missions it is of critical importance that a proper legal framework be in place at the outset when the military arrive, followed by the international police. If this can be done the likelihood of success in creating a system of justice will be greater, the chances of the most violent and criminalized elements filling the vacuum will be reduced, and the tension between the need to maintain order and at the same time apply international standards will be lessened. There are things that can be done ahead of time to cut down on the number of problems faced by police when they arrive.

1. There must be clarity as to the legal framework of the mission. As far as possible, given that no one can become fully versed in a foreign legal system in a short period of time, personnel must know and understand the legal framework before deployment. Standby codes and standard operating procedures for the emergency phase, on which international police could be trained and certified, could greatly facilitate this. These codes and procedures must meet international standards and be capable of being implemented in a post-conflict environment where it is likely that there will be a lack of security, resources and personnel.

2. Before deployment, international police must understand the political context, the nature of the conflict that brought them to the region, the nature of the criminal elements and cases they are likely to find and the culture that they will be working in.

3. Policing must be viewed as part of a rule-of-law continuum which includes the judiciary (courts and prosecutors) and the penal or correctional institutions. Practitioners from each area, with field experience, must be part of all planning in relation to the legal framework and implementation of that framework.

4. In executive missions, capacity building must begin from 'day one'. Active dialogue must take place between the international and local actors in relation to establishing or re-establishing the judicial system. Local expertise and acceptance are crucial.

5. Given the short rotations of international police and the diversity of the legal systems from which they come, critical areas such as war crimes, crimes against humanity, organized crime and other sensitive crime issues require the creation of a cadre of police who are specially trained and equipped, sent for longer rotations and provided with adequate guidelines and procedures.

6. As part of respecting local input and learning from it, it is important to incorporate traditional dispute resolution systems within the international legal framework.

7. A system of accountability for international police which includes clearly defined rules and procedures must be established and in place at the outset of a mission.

8. The civilian police authorities and the military must have standing systems of coordination and information sharing from the outset. Memoranda of understanding or agreements in areas such as report contents, evidence transfers, detention and search would help in this regard.

3. Policing from above: executive policing and peace implementation in Kosovo

Michael J. Dziedzic

I. Introduction

Not only has the focus of peace operations shifted since the end of the cold war from conflict between states to conflict within them, but the threshold for intervention in internal conflict has also been steadily lowered. Consequently, when the UN Interim Administration Mission in Kosovo (UNMIK) assumed responsibility for law enforcement in Kosovo in June 1999, the processes of peacemaking, peace enforcement and economic reconstruction were just beginning. The capacity of the UNMIK Police to establish and maintain public security had significant ramifications for each of these aspects of peace implementation. Executive policing by UNMIK was also intended to provide a basis for developing the rule of law, an essential underpinning for an enduring peace.

This chapter examines these four areas of peace implementation—peacemaking, peace enforcement, economic reconstruction and institutionalizing the rule of law—to illustrate the contributions of executive policing to each. First, however, it is necessary to appreciate how very different the new environment for peace operations is and why executive policing has not merely filled a temporary gap in public security but has played a strategic role in forging a peace that can be sustained.[1]

II. The international context

During the cold war multilateral peacekeeping was used primarily to monitor compliance with agreements to end conflict between states and had certain characteristics that shaped the way peace implementation was carried out:

[1] This chapter draws on the 4 stages of peace implementation examined in Covey, J., Dziedzic, M. and Hawley, L. (eds), *The Quest for Peaceful Co-existence in Kosovo: Evolving Strategies of Peace Implementation* (Lynn Rienner: Boulder, Colo., forthcoming).

1. The conflict itself had to be *'ripe' for a negotiated solution*, meaning that the parties recognized the declining utility of the use of force and were reconciled to the need for international intervention.

2. The process was *linear or sequential*. The diplomatic phase had to be successfully concluded; then military peacekeepers could be deployed to monitor compliance with the peace that the diplomats had hammered out.

3. Because of this, civilian and military peacekeepers had *discrete tasks* that were largely independent of each other.

4. The presence of peacekeepers was entirely at the sufferance of the parties to the dispute, which meant that the UN's 'blue helmets' had to conduct themselves with strict *neutrality*.

One of the hallmarks of the current international system is that intra-state conflict has become a leading source of international disorder. Even as the international community has sought to adapt and develop a proper set of tools to manage troubled states, the magnitude and difficulty of the task have greatly expanded. The complexity of the tasks to be performed has vastly increased as the threshold for intervention has been lowered.

If it ever made sense to wait for a failing state to complete the descent into chaos and become ripe for international intervention, the holocaust in Rwanda must surely have disabused most policy makers of the advisability of this prescription. Subsequently in Kosovo a coercive bombing campaign rather than a diplomatic process of negotiation created conditions for the introduction of the peace force—the Kosovo Force (KFOR).

The deployment of UNMIK marked not the culmination of peacemaking but rather a continuation of the internal conflict by other means. Under such circumstances, peacemaking, peacekeeping and peace building must take place simultaneously, and civilian and military peace implementers can only move the peace process forward if they forge an effective partnership. One prominent lesson derived from the Bosnia experience has been that neutrality is folly in the face of resistance by local political power brokers who are committed to the use of violence to prevent the international mandate being fulfilled.[2] This merely prolongs the international presence, and when

[2] Stedman, S., 'Spoiler problems in peace processes', eds Paul C. Stern and Daniel Druckman, *International Conflict Resolution After the Cold War* (National Academy Press: Washington, DC, 2000), pp. 178–224.

military peacekeepers eventually seek to depart the conditions for renewed instability will prevail. Thus, a new principle has emerged to guide peace implementation in fractured states: support those who support the peace process and actively oppose those who obstruct it.

In Kosovo (and East Timor), moreover, the UN had to reinvent itself as a surrogate government even as it sought to build capacity for local rule. It became responsible for law and order.

In sum, executive policing has taken place in a context which in many fundamental ways is a reversal of the conditions confronted during the cold war.

1. Since waiting for internal conflict to become 'ripe' for international intervention may leave minority populations excruciatingly vulnerable, *military intervention has taken place before there is a peace to keep.*

2. The peacemaking phase has just begun when military intervention is initiated. Consequently, diplomats, military peacekeepers, international civilian police (CivPols), civilian peace builders from international organizations and non-governmental organizations (NGOs), and other members of the international community *pursue their functions simultaneously throughout most of the mission.*

3. Owing to this simultaneity and the need to confront spoilers, *civilian and military entities are highly dependent on each other* for the success of their efforts.

4. A neutral posture towards local actors who seek to obstruct the peace process through violence and intimidation has proved to be a formula for paralysis. Peace implementers have recognized the need to take *active measures to support those who support the peace and sanction those who oppose it.*

5. The international intervention may confront a void in law enforcement from the very outset of the mission, and self-sustaining peace will ultimately hinge on *establishing the rule of law.*

III. Peace implementation in Kosovo

The Kosovo case is especially useful for illustrating the strategic contributions that executive policing may be called upon to make. The situation the international community encountered there in June 1999 had to be transformed in fundamental ways before peace could become enduring.

The peacemakers faced unresolved conflicts on two fronts. To make peace, UNMIK had to demilitarize the conflict between the Kosovar Albanians and Serbs and avert a civil war between former members of the Kosovo Liberation Army (KLA), led by Hashim Thaci, and the Democratic League of Kosovo (LDK) of Ibrahim Rugova. In the long run the objective was to transform these conflicts from violent, 'zero-sum' struggles into political contests that would be pursued through peaceful, democratic means ('from bullets to ballots').

The *peace enforcement* challenge for KFOR and, over time, for the UNMIK Police came in the form of political extremists linked with transnational criminal activity. The interests of these parallel, often informal power structures were opposed to the peace process and they exercised a dominant influence over the body politic in both the Kosovar Albanian and the Serb communities. Securing such an environment required establishing a monopoly on the legitimate use of force and taking active measures to marginalize or defeat the sources of political violence.

Economic reconstruction required that the political economy be transformed from its criminalized condition, dominated by 'grey' (i.e., smuggling) and black market transactions. Illicit sources of wealth sustained not only transnational criminal activity but also shadowy networks of security agents and hit squads. The aim was not to eradicate all criminal activity, which would be impossible: rather, revenue obtained from illicit activity should no longer be able to determine who governs and how. There was a need to break the overweening influence that criminal elements had over the political process and to stimulate a free-market economy that could out-compete the black market.

For the *rule of law* to prevail, the police, judiciary and penal system which had traditionally served the state as instruments of political control had to be transformed. These institutions had to begin to function in a way that delivered public security and justice on behalf of all of society, respecting human rights and treating all citizens equally. They had to be perceived by former combatants as sufficiently capable and just for violence not to re-emerge as the preferred option for change.

Executive policing can have strategic significance for each of these processes. This theme is developed below for each of the four aspects of peace implementation identified. The nature of the challenge is

described, the general process involved in fostering these transforma-
tions is described and, finally, the contributions that executive
policing has made, or has failed to make, are discussed.

Executive policing and peacemaking

The challenge

The context in Kosovo after June 1999 was clearly not a 'post-
conflict' one. UNMIK was confronted by unresolved conflicts on two
fronts.

First, Serb and Albanian factions continued to harbour incompatible
aspirations regarding Kosovo's 'final status'. Progress on this front
was held hostage to the outcome of the clash between Slobodan
Milosevic, then President of the Federal Republic of Yugoslavia
(FRY), and the international community. As long as Milosevic
retained the capacity to manipulate the Serb population in Kosovo,
peaceful coexistence was virtually impossible. The best UNMIK
could do initially was to preserve a viable option for Serbs to continue
to live in Kosovo while buying time for Milosevic's removal from
office and his eventual extradition to The Hague to be engineered.

The second front was an internecine struggle within the Kosovar
Albanian body politic. The usurpation of power by the KLA after June
1999 created a volatile confrontation with followers of Rugova who,
for most of the previous decade, had operated a parallel government in
passive resistance to Milosevic's rule. Preventing this intramural conflict from erupting into civil war was one of UNMIK's most crucial
early challenges.

The response

UNMIK followed a strategy of progressively incorporating key elites
into a process of peacemaking. The ability to wield credible inducements and sanctions to support those who supported UN Security
Council Resolution 1244 and oppose those who sought to impede it
was essential for success. This strategy, as articulated and implemented by the Principal Deputy Special Representative of the
Secretary General (PDSRSG), Jock Covey, was incremental in nature.
Over time, as the more tractable disputes were resolved, confidence

was built among an increasing number of power brokers, enabling more challenging issues to be resolved.

The components of UNMIK's peacemaking strategy during the first 18 months of the mission were as follows.

1. *Dialogue among former disputants.* The first step in this process is to persuade political rivals to talk to each other.

2. *Confidence-building measures.* There are two dimensions to confidence building. One involves the relationship between the international community and each of the parties to the dispute. The peace mission builds confidence by demonstrating that it is impartial and able to satisfy basic needs, especially public security. Local elites are expected to reciprocate by working with the international community to isolate extremists and mobilize public support for the peace process. The second dimension pertains to the disputants themselves. The international community helps to build confidence among former combatant groups by ensuring that their agreements are implemented faithfully.

3. *Reassessment of political objectives.* The parties to the conflict must eventually be persuaded to reassess their incompatible goals. This can be encouraged through the judicious application of both 'carrots' and 'sticks'. On the one hand, inducements are intended to show that long-term material and social interests are better served by cooperation with the peace process. On the other hand, sanctions should demonstrate that obstructing the peace process by violent means is a path to self-destruction. The most crucial component is the capacity to enforce the law and bring spoilers to justice when they use force to obstruct the peace process. The international community must have both capabilities at its disposal in order to coax the parties down this path.

4. *Risk-taking.* Local leaders who decide to cooperate will need the support of the international community in coping with the risks that are associated with doing so. The gravest threats are likely to come from hard-liners within their own faction who regard the moderation of their original war aims as a betrayal of the cause.

5. *Formalize gains and repeat process.* Each incremental step should be consolidated with an agreement, election or formal undertaking of some sort. The process of demilitarizing the KLA, for example, was consolidated with the creation of a civil emergency force, the Kosovo Protection Corps (KPC), of which former KLA

members provided the core. A key step in averting open conflict between Rugova and Thaci came in December 1999 with the agreement to create the Joint Interim Administrative Structure (JIAS) which began to supplant the 'parallel structures' established by the KLA. The Kosovo-wide elections held in November 2001 were a major step in bringing the Kosovo Serb leadership into the process.

The contributions of executive policing

Dialogue among former disputants. The initial absence of an executive policing capability (because of the inevitable time lag in recruiting and deploying international civilian police) contributed to the inability to prevent 'ethnic cleansing', this time against the Serb population. Initially, KFOR and the UNMIK Police[3] were unable to assert control over the campaign of violence against the Serb population, resulting in a major exodus of Serbs from Kosovo during the first months of the mission. This greatly compounded the challenge of enticing political leaders from the Kosovar Serb community even to engage in a dialogue. It took almost a year before Bishop Artimje, patriarch of the Serb Orthodox Church in Kosovo, agreed to provide what amounted to token Serb representation in the deliberative processes taking place within the JIAS, established by UNMIK as a means of involving the local population in the governance of Kosovo.

Confidence-building measures. By virtue of their very presence on the streets, international civilian police should help to return a post-conflict population to normality by increasing popular trust in the role of the international community and by deterring crime.

Risk-taking. Artimje took considerable risk whenever he left his monastic enclave in Gracanica. This required UNMIK Police to provide a close protection detail for the bishop and his representatives when they travelled to meetings at UNMIK headquarters in Pristina or other events related to the peace process. Personnel with the specialized skills and experience required for this duty were recruited from the rank and file of the UNMIK Police to create a Close Protection Unit (CPU). They were in demand not only for this purpose but also to provide personal security to visiting dignitaries, as would be the case for any government. The number of UNMIK Police who were qualified for this function was not adequate to meet the demand,

---

[3] On the UNMIK Police's relationship to KFOR see chapter 2, section I1, in this volume.

however. As a partial solution, once Special Police Units (SPUs) were deployed in the summer of 2000, members of the Jordanian SPU were trained to assist CPU details with some basic aspects of VIP security.[4]

Formalize gains and repeat process. KFOR and the UNMIK Police confronted a crucial public security challenge in preventing campaign violence from derailing the October 2000 municipal elections. As the campaign was about to begin numerous incidents of intimidation and a series of armed assaults, including assassination, began to take place, aimed primarily at members of Rugova's LDK. The UNMIK Police had nowhere near the number of personnel trained in close protection that would be needed to provide bodyguard service for all endangered candidates. Moreover, this was not the most constructive precedent to set since candidates in future campaigns would feel entitled to surround themselves with an entourage of bodyguards, defeating the aim of demilitarizing politics. To develop a response, KFOR and the UNMIK Police formed a task force to assess which candidates were at risk. They then coordinated their patrolling to provide a regular presence near those candidates' homes and campaign sites, as well as offering a number of other security measures.

These steps, coupled with the threat of disqualification for any political parties and candidates who were shown to be responsible for campaign violence, allowed the electoral process to unfold in relative tranquillity. Rugova and his politics of non-violence came out on top in the municipal elections, garnering almost 60 per cent of the vote; parties associated with the KLA also obtained a major stake in the system with 35 per cent of the vote. This set in motion a process whereby power at the municipal level could begin to be exercised by elected local officials as opposed to de facto parallel structures.

Executive policing and peace enforcement

The challenge

In June 1999, as the KLA moved quickly to fill the power vacuum created by the departure of Serb security forces, UNMIK had scarcely begun to organize the international civilian mission. Thus KFOR carried the initial burden of trying to avert ethnic cleansing, this time with the Kosovo Serb population as the intended victims. Milosevic's

---

[4] On the role of the SPUs see also chapter 5, section II, in this volume.

Interior Ministry Police also remained active, fomenting violent resistance to the peace process in Mitrovica and Strpce, and maintaining a base for terrorist activity in Gracanica. Politically motivated violence took a variety of forms, the most significant being intimidation, assassination of political rivals, terrorism against minority enclaves, orchestrated civil disturbances, and insurrection in southern Serbia and Macedonia.

The response[5]

British troops were widely regarded as the most effective at responding to political violence, having institutionalized lessons drawn from the Malaysian counter-insurgency campaign, Northern Ireland and similar experiences. The essence of their strategy for enforcing peace was to shape the environment by finding, 'fixing' in place and then striking at spoilers who use violence to disrupt the peace process. Essential to this strategy was the establishment of a framework of operations involving both military and international police capabilities.

Finding. Once the operational framework was established, troops and international police were in a position to obtain information from the population and exploit other means of identifying the sources of politically motivated violence.

Fixing. The collective network of military installations, police stations, patrolling, checkpoints, point security and passive security measures was used to limit the freedom of movement and disruptive activities of spoilers. The formation of the KPC was another measure that was intended to 'strategically fix' former KLA combatants.

Striking. Rather than continuously reacting to symptoms of the problem, the British approach emphasizes striking at the sources of political violence. This requires close collaboration with the political authority managing the mission to determine which local actors should be regarded as spoilers and when coercion can be used without jeopardizing local consent.

[5] This section draws extensively on Lovelock, B. (Lt-Col), 'Securing peace: defeating political violence', eds Covey, Dziedzic and Hawley (note 1).

Table 3.1. Sources of capabilities for the security framework in Kosovo

	KFOR	MSU/SPU	UNMIK Police
Fixed checkpoints	X	X	
Mobile checkpoints	X	X	X
Foot patrols	X	X	X
Mounted patrols	X	X	X
Traffic control			X
Crowd control	X	X	
Fixed police stations			X
Mobile police stations		X	

Note: KFOR = Kosovo Force; MSU = Multinational Specialized Unit; SPU = Special Police Unit; UNMIK = UN Mission in Kosovo.

The contributions of executive policing

Finding. The capabilities used by the UNMIK Police to find the perpetrators of political violence include criminal investigations and forensics. KFOR also has at its disposal technical intelligence, human intelligence and surveillance. British forces place particular emphasis on interaction with the local population. KFOR's Multinational Specialized Unit (MSU), made up primarily of Italian *carabinieri* with vast institutional experience in dealing with the Mafia, is also especially well suited for this purpose.[6]

The challenge was to find a way to exploit the criminal intelligence of KFOR and the UNMIK Police so that effective law enforcement action could be taken by the UNMIK Police. In late 1999 the 'Quint countries'[7] decided to create a Criminal Intelligence Unit (CIU) for this purpose within the UNMIK Police. A facility was constructed for the CIU at KFOR headquarters, affording both security and proximity to the Quint countries' national intelligence analysts. For more than a year, however, the CIU was hampered by concerns in certain intelligence circles about sharing classified information even among the Quint countries. Other institutional barriers to its effectiveness included the need for KFOR and UNMIK to collaborate to establish investigative priorities and procedures to convert intelligence into a useful guide for criminal investigations by the UNMIK Police.

[6] On the MSU in Kosovo, see chapter 5, section II., in this volume.
[7] France, Germany, Italy, the UK and the USA.

Specialists assigned to the CIU also require a sophisticated knowledge of the relevant local personalities, cultural considerations, Kosovo's political dynamics, and the strengths and weaknesses of the international and local organizations involved. This can only come with periods of duty far longer than the typical UNMIK policeman (normally six months) or KFOR soldier (six months).

Fixing. The capabilities required to construct the framework of operations are shared by KFOR and the UNMIK Police. Adding to the complexity, both have military police entities. The MSU belongs to KFOR and the SPUs come under UNMIK.

Passive security measures are a cost-effective means of fixing spoilers. Measures taken by UNMIK Police and KFOR included street lighting in high-threat areas, barriers to slow or stop traffic, and alternatives to existing traffic patterns, such as the building of by-pass roads and dusk-to-dawn closure of non-essential access routes.

The creation of the KPC and, to a lesser extent, the Kosovo Police Service (KPS) were part of a long-term process aimed at strategically fixing the KLA, depoliticizing it and integrating individual KLA members into civil society. Some senior KPC commanders have continued to act with impunity, however, and have proved impervious to efforts to discipline them. Rogue ex-KLA members are widely regarded as having been catalysts in the insurrections that erupted in southern Serbia in 2000 and subsequently in Macedonia in early 2001.

Striking. Operations must be carefully focused, using the most appropriate security element available to deal with the task at hand. This involved activities by KFOR such as cordon and search operations to seize arms and illegal materials. The UNMIK Police established an elite unit for high-risk arrests that was used in operations targeting spoilers, often with KFOR back-up. Politically motivated violence may also include orchestrated civil disturbances, especially in response to operations of the sort described above. Thus, crowd and riot control units are also required. This was why SPUs were recruited and assigned to the UNMIK Police. Striking effectively at spoilers also involves the use of an information campaign to nurture the confidence and support of the local population.

Perhaps the most serious shortcoming for the international community was the chronic inability to develop admissible evidence in high-profile episodes of politically motivated violence. One notorious case involved the remote-controlled bombing of a bus from Nis, which killed 15 people. Although three suspects were arrested on the basis of intelligence gathered by KFOR, this could not be used in court.[8] Failure to bring spoilers to justice undermines UNMIK's capacity to encourage the disputants to reassess their objectives and take risks for peace, since it has demonstrable difficulty imposing effective sanctions on those who seek to destroy the peace process.

Executive policing and economic reconstruction

The challenge[9]

The disintegration of the former Yugoslavia's centrally planned economic model, entrenched communist-era cronyism and transnational criminal networks have interacted in Kosovo to create a criminalized political economy. When Milosevic stripped Kosovo of its autonomy in 1989, Kosovar Albanian managers, supervisors and university professors were replaced by Serbs. Many families survived on remittances from sons who were sent to Europe to find employment. Some turned to criminal activity, particularly heroin trafficking and prostitution. Kosovar gangs began to displace indigenous criminal enterprises throughout Europe, in part because they were ruthless and their obscure language and insular nature made them impervious to penetration by law enforcement agencies. Ethnic connections also facilitated transnational cooperation with the criminal underworld in Albania and Macedonia. As early as 1994 a drugs-for-guns connection was discernible involving the shipment of heroin and other contraband through Albania, Kosovo and Macedonia. A return flow of arms went into Albanian ports and from there to Kosovo.[10]

Managers installed by Milosevic proceeded to plunder state-owned enterprises for personal gain, including stripping assets from the Trepca mining complex. Under Marshal Josip Broz Tito, the components of Yugoslavia's industrial economy—from extraction of raw

---

[8] On the problem of developing court-admissible evidence, see chapter 2, sections II and III, in this volume.

[9] This section is drawn from a discussion of Kosovo's political economy co-authored with Phil Williams in a forthcoming US Institute of Peace Special Report, 'Lawless rule vs rule of law in the Balkans'.

[10] See, e.g., Hisloper, R., 'The calm before the storm? The influence of cross-border networks, corruption, and contraband on Macedonian stability and regional security', Paper presented at the 2001 Annual Meeting of the American Political Science Association, San Francisco, Calif., 2001.

materials to processing, production and distribution—had been disbursed among the various republics to promote political stability. This industrial complex disintegrated into isolated and dysfunctional components as Yugoslavia's republics broke away. Economic sanctions imposed on Yugoslavia gave further impetus for socially tolerated criminal gangs to operate as sanctions-busters during the wars and in their aftermath. People became dependent on smuggling for fuel, food and other consumer items.

Kosovo's already crumbling infrastructure was further devastated by the reign of terror that generated the exodus of refugees in 1998–99, by NATO's bombing campaign, and subsequently by retribution against the Serbs. Serb workers abandoned their jobs, rendering even the most basic utilities, such as water and power, inoperative. When the peace mission began in June 1999, with the exception of small-scale retail trade, Kosovo's formal economy was in a state of collapse, and unemployment was estimated to be 70 per cent.[11] Lacking opportunities in the formal economy, many Kosovars turned to the underground economy as the only alternative. There were gradations of involvement, beginning with purchase of 'grey-market' commodities at cheaper prices than in the legal economy and selling smuggled cigarettes and other contraband.

The void in law enforcement after June 1999 turned Kosovo into a sanctuary for crime. The influx of international assistance was a further inducement for establishing criminal operations there. As a result, Kosovo's economy became increasingly enmeshed in the underground economy of the Balkans. Extremist elements were involved in trafficking in drugs and other contraband and in arms smuggling networks, and proved adept at exploiting political grievances among the region's ethnic Albanian populations to fuel inter-ethnic conflict.

The response

The formal economy.[12] The 'white' or formal economy needs to generate an alternative source of income and employment that can compete with and displace the black economy.

---

[11] International Crisis Group, *Kosovo Spring: The International Crisis Group Guide to Kosovo* (International Crisis Group: Brussels, 1998), p. 62.

[12] In the formal economy, transactions for goods and services are recorded and conducted openly. In the 'grey' economy, they are kept off the public record to avoid taxation or other

The grey economy. Revenue generated by the grey or smuggling economy needs to be captured by the state. This serves the dual purpose of funding essential government activities (such as public security) while depriving criminal elements of one of their principal sources of revenue. A regime of taxation and law enforcement needs to be established that makes it more cost-effective to pay customs duties and similar taxes than to seek to avoid them.

The black economy. Political extremists sustained by earnings from criminal activity have created parallel power structures that must be dealt with if peace is to endure. The peacemaking and peace enforcement strategies described previously serve this purpose, if executed successfully, by severing the nexus between illicit wealth and political power. To prevent the re-emergence of organized crime and political extremism as dominant political forces, it is also necessary to develop the rule of law (discussed in the next section). To the extent that these three strategies flourish, and alternatives in the formal economy can be generated, the transformation from a criminalized to a legitimate political economy can take place.

The contributions of executive policing

The formal economy. Although Kosovo is not blessed with natural resources, it does have extensive mineral deposits that have been exploited since the days of the Roman Empire. Known as the Trepca mining complex, the mines, refineries and smelters were located on both sides of the ethnic divide.

The headquarters and a major smelter were situated at Zvecan in the north of Kosovo, which remained effectively under Serb 'parallel' governance. When the lead smelter resumed operating in mid-2000, the absence of functioning environmental protective measures meant that dense clouds of harmful lead smoke engulfed Mitrovica, forcing UNMIK and KFOR to act. Before seizing control of the smelter, however, UNMIK secured financing to conduct environmental clean-up and a technical assessment of the economic potential of the entire complex. The UNMIK Police played a supporting role in the actual operation, but the subsequent task of providing security and preventing sabotage was turned over to the SPU. This action made it possible

---

forms of government regulation, and consumer goods are obtained through smuggling. In the black economy transactions for goods and services are objectionable on moral grounds as well as being illegal. Typical consumer goods are not involved.

to begin assessing the potential contribution of Kosovo's mining industry to the formal economy, as well as asserting a measure of political authority over northern Kosovo.

The grey economy. The Zvecan operation also contributed to UNMIK's capacity to regulate the grey economy. For the first time the UNMIK Police began controlling traffic across the boundary between Kosovo and Serbia. This was a vital step in the direction of asserting UNMIK's authority to collect customs revenue on commerce from Serbia. Earlier the UNMIK Police had begun collecting customs duties on the five border crossings with Macedonia and Montenegro. Related to this was the executive policing function of patrolling the borders and smuggling routes used to circumvent customs collection points. The border patrol mission was only one of many paramilitary tasks performed by the SPU.

The black economy. The influx of 'internationals' was followed by the proliferation of brothels in Kosovo and related trafficking in women. While the UNMIK Police strove to clamp down on this, individual CivPols were among the patrons of these illicit establishments. Part of the black market revenue that feeds the criminal–extremist linkage is therefore provided by the international community.

Executive policing and institutionalizing the rule of law

The challenge

Both the Serb administrative apparatus and the traditional Albanian 'parallel' governmental structures had largely disappeared by July 1999. This included the institutions of public security. There were no police, judges or prisons to provide law and order and even the basic infrastructure was lacking. The main prison at Istock, for example, with a capacity for 1200 inmates, had been bombed during the air campaign and was unusable. A climate of lawlessness prevailed as those who possessed arms took advantage of the situation to acquire property, take revenge on Serbs or both. A lack of border controls allowed smuggling to take place virtually unchecked.

Except for humanitarian activities, UNMIK required many months to mobilize the personnel and financial resources to begin filling the gap in services and public security. The refusal of Kosovar Albanian judges to administer the legal code that had been associated with post-

1989 Serb rule[13] paralysed the judicial system for the remainder of 1999. The consequence of this early void in law enforcement was that organized crime and political extremism were able to gain a powerful grip over Kosovar society. Together these mutually reinforcing influences represented an 'uncivil society' that was united by its interest in undermining efforts to institutionalize the rule of law.

The criminalization of Kosovo's political economy is a grave threat to the embryonic political and judicial systems being established there. This danger is perhaps best illustrated by the wave of commercial construction that took place after June 1999, particularly in Pristina. In addition to being an attractive way for criminal enterprises to launder money, many of these structures were built illegally on municipal property. When UNMIK began to clamp down by demolishing illegal buildings in the autumn of 2000, Rexhep Luci, the official in the Pristina municipality responsible for the enforcement of permit requirements, was assassinated by an organized crime 'hit team'.[14]

The response

Capacity building. When, as in Kosovo, existing institutions have completely collapsed, international personnel must perform their functions initially—in this case, KFOR and the UNMIK Police. The next step is to develop the local capacity to maintain order, enforce law and adjudicate disputes. Capacity building, therefore, needs to be holistic, addressing the complete spectrum of institutions involved— the legal code, judiciary, police and penal system.

Safeguards. Effective safeguards must be developed within both the state and civil society to ensure that institutions perform in a manner that is accountable to the public and applicable to all. Safeguards involve the capacity both to observe the performance of personnel and to sanction misconduct. Structural safeguards within the state, such as political pluralism, open elections that permit transitions of power and judicial autonomy, are part of the answer. It is also essential to create independent oversight bodies with effective disciplinary mechanisms for each institution involved in the rule of law in order to promote

---

[13] See chapter 2, section II, in this volume.

[14] 'Attacks against prominent Kosovars lead to renewed efforts to stem violence', *UNMIK News*, no. 19 (Sep. 2000), available at URL <http://www.unmikonline.org/pub/news/nl59. html>.

transparency and accountability. These must be matched by vigorous safeguards in civil society, such as a free press (especially investigative journalism), civic organizations devoted to ensuring human rights and clean government, and education of the public about their rights and mechanisms for redress of abuses.

Partnership. The timing of the transition to local 'ownership' should be determined by the capacity of local institutions and by the strength of domestic safeguards. Capacity building will invariably be accomplished before local safeguards are able to function reliably. A period of partnership with international personnel will therefore probably be required after local personnel have been trained in order to permit domestic safeguards to develop and be tested successfully before full responsibility is transferred. If this critical gap is not filled, these institutions will almost certainly remain vulnerable, if not already beholden, to political extremists and criminal networks. As the level of risk is reduced to a tolerable level, local police, prosecutors and judges can be given increasingly prominent roles in handling the most sensitive cases.

The contributions of executive policing

Capacity building. Responsibility for training the new KPS was assigned to the Organization for Security and Co-operation in Europe (OSCE). Although it has been a challenge to recruit minorities to serve in the KPS, the OSCE has managed to create a multi-ethnic force that is representative of the population of Kosovo. After KPS personnel graduated from training in the Kosovo Police Service School (KPSS), they spent about three months under the tutelage of an UNMIK Police Field Training Officer before being assigned to a permanent police station. On-the-job training was a weakness, since UNMIK Police were not recruited with this function in mind. As a result, many of those assigned to mentor graduates of the police academy had no aptitude for field training and some were not good role models.[15]

Safeguards. When safeguards have collapsed or are non-existent, as in Kosovo, interim international safeguards will be necessary. Since the UNMIK Police have executive policing authority, it has been possible to develop the KPS leadership in a progressive, graduated

---

[15] See chapter 6, section II, in this volume.

manner under their tutelage. Beginning in the autumn of 2000, the first KPS personnel were assigned to their permanent police stations. To ensure the progressive transformation of the culture of law enforcement, the final phase of an executive policing mission should entail the placement of seasoned international police officers alongside Kosovar police chiefs and other senior officials as both mentors and monitors.

The capacity of the UNMIK Police to imbue the KPS with an ethos of public service and respect for human rights is directly correlated with the conduct and professionalism of its own personnel. International police must lead by example. It is difficult for the UN to avoid fielding police who are poor role models, in part because it must recruit on a global basis and cannot exclude personnel from UN member states that are themselves repressive and authoritarian. It is even unable to hold the UNMIK Police to the same standard as the local personnel, because as internationals they have immunity from local law.[16]

Partnership. In addition to the senior managers described above, other components of UNMIK Police that could contribute essential capabilities to a longer-term partnership are the CIU, the CPU, the high-risk arrest team and the crowd control capability of the SPUs or the MSU. A sophisticated criminal investigative capability will also be needed.

IV. Conclusions

In Kosovo, the exercise of executive policing powers by the UNMIK Police has been relevant for the four components of peace implementation. The nature of the impact has varied, however, and, in some circumstances it has not been constructive. In those cases where executive policing has actually detracted from peace implementation, this has generally been due to the failure of member states to respond in a timely fashion when a mission was established or to ensure that the personal and professional conduct of the personnel provided met the minimum standards.

Peacemaking. On the positive side of the ledger, the initial dialogue between Kosovo's Albanian and Serb communities would probably have been impossible without the security the CPU provided to

[16] See also chapter 2, section IV, in this volume.

Bishop Artimje and his key advisers. The municipal elections of October 2000, moreover, locked in gains made by peacemakers in averting a civil war between rival Kosovar Albanian factions and undercut the power of 'parallel' structures at the municipal level. This would not have been possible without close collaboration between the UNMIK Police and KFOR to ensure that the electoral campaign was not disrupted by violence.

On the other hand, the time lag in recruiting and deploying international civilian police created an initial public security gap. It was during this period that the worst violence against the Serb population took place, permitting a process of ethnic cleansing that made UNMIK's task of preserving a multi-ethnic state and making peace between Kosovo's Albanian and Serb communities even more daunting.

Peace enforcement. The UNMIK Police, working together with KFOR as part of the overall framework of operations, were essential for peace enforcement. The first requirement in defeating political violence is to develop intelligence on perpetrators of violence and their networks. The formation of the CIU was a major innovation in this regard, even though it continued to confront vexing challenges. The process of de-legitimizing the use of political violence by incorporating former KLA members into the KPC and the KPS served the strategic aim of fixing the former rebel group in place. Finally, the UNMIK Police provided a crucial high-risk arrest capability for operations mounted to strike at prominent political spoilers. Their most serious shortcoming was the chronic inability to develop admissible evidence in high-profile episodes of politically motivated violence.

Economic reconstruction. One potential source of employment in the formal economy was the Trepca mining complex. After UNMIK and KFOR acted to wrest control of the headquarters and other vital components from Milosevic's cronies, SPUs of the UNMIK Police were used to provide security and prevent sabotage of the facility. This operation also contributed to UNMIK's capacity to regulate the grey economy. However, the presence of UNMIK Police had a counterproductive impact on the black economy: as mentioned above, international police were among the patrons of brothels run by Kosovo's criminal underworld.

Institutionalizing the rule of law. The limitations of the UNMIK Police in nurturing the rule of law have exposed the inadequacy of the recruitment process for international police. Although the KPSS was universally regarded as highly professional, on-the-job training by the UNMIK Police was not. To imbue the graduates of the KPSS with an ethos of public service and respect for human rights, international police should lead by example. Too often, this is not possible.

In contrast to the varying calibre of the UNMIK Police, the CPU high-risk arrest team and the CIU and SPUs were staffed by individuals who were highly skilled in their functional specialisms. Only those who could demonstrate the capacity to perform the tasks required were able to join these units. This suggests that, as the role of international community in policing evolves toward a partnership relationship, a different recruitment mechanism will be required. To ensure the progressive transformation of the culture of law enforcement, the final phase of an executive policing mission should entail the placement of seasoned international police officers alongside Kosovar police chiefs and other senior officials as both mentors and monitors.

4. Policing from below: community policing as an objective in peace operations

*Eirin Mobekk**

I. Introduction

Community policing has been, if not always an expressed objective, at least part of some of the most recent peace operations, such as those in Bosnia, Kosovo and East Timor. In East Timor, the use of community policing by the United Nations civilian police (CivPols) was a declared goal.[1] However, it is an elusive concept and its applicability in the context of international peace operations needs examination. This is particularly pertinent where the police mission includes a law enforcement mandate—not only training and monitoring—as was the case in both Kosovo and East Timor. This chapter deals with community policing in peace operations where the CivPol component has a law enforcement mandate—executive policing.

This chapter makes extensive reference to the case of East Timor but takes a more general approach when discussing the possibility and indeed the usefulness of applying the concept of community policing in peace operations. The inherent problems with the term and the ways in which these problems translate from a national to an international context are outlined. The chapter looks not only at the potential for and the limitations of the use of community policing by

---

[1] United Nations Transitional Administration in East Timor (UNTAET), 'UNTAET CivPol administration and operations manual' (undated).

* The interviews on which this chapter is partly based were conducted as part of a research project funded by the John D. and Catherine T. MacArthur Foundation. The project resulted in a report, 'Policing peace operations: United Nations civilian police in East Timor', Monograph for the John D. and Catherine T. MacArthur Foundation Program on Peace and International Co-operation, King's College, London, Oct. 2001. Representatives of the UN CivPols, UNTAET and East Timorese civil society in Dili and in different districts throughout East Timor were interviewed in Mar. and Apr. 2001, and interviews with UNTAET and CivPol representatives were conducted in London and New York between Nov. 2000 and July 2001. All have been kept confidential.

international forces maintaining law and order but also at the value of teaching local forces to use community policing.

II. Community policing: a contested concept

Community policing is an essentially contested concept.

The International Association of Chiefs of Police defines community policing as 'a philosophy that guides an entire police department's approach to policing . . . The law enforcement works in partnership with a community to solve the problems of crime and disorder. A police department must be pro-active, reaching out to a community with whom it will work'.[2]

However, community policing has become a 'buzz word', often used by professionals and academics to substitute for terms such as crime prevention, foot patrol, police–community relations and so on.[3] It has been used interchangeably with problem-oriented policing and problem-solving policing.[4] It has been used to describe 'horse patrols, neighbourhood police offices, intensified enforcement of drunk-driving laws, prompt response to emergency calls for service, tightened disciplinary procedures, statements of departmental values and objectives, liaison with ethnic groups, victim support'.[5] It has been defined as existing when police 'transform communities from being passive consumers of police protection to active co-producers of public safety'.[6] It has been argued to include the 'total organisational commitment involving police, social services and citizens of the community coming together to identify and find solutions to local problems'.[7] The concept means different things to different people,

[2] Thayer, R. and Reynolds, M., 'Community oriented policing', *Journal of Planning Literature*, vol. 12, no. 1 (Aug. 1997), p. 93.

[3] Friedmann, R., *Community Policing: Comparative Perspectives and Prospects* (Harvester/Wheatsheaf: London, 1992), p. 2. On different uses of the term see also Wycoff, M. A., 'The benefits of community policing: evidence and conjecture', eds J. Greene and S. Mastrofski, *Community Policing: Rhetoric or Reality* (Praeger: New York, 1988), pp. 103–107.

[4] Trojanowicz, R. and Bucqueroux, B., *Community Policing: A Contemporary Perspective*, (Anderson Publishing: Cincinnati, Ohio, 1990), pp. 6–8.

[5] Bayley, D., 'International differences in community policing', ed. D. Rosenbaum, *The Challenge of Community Policing: Testing the Promises* (Sage: London, 1994), p. 278.

[6] Bayley, D. and Shearing, C., 'The future of policing', *Law and Society Review*, vol. 30, no. 3 (1996), p. 585.

[7] Pouliot, N., 'Armed CIVPOL in policing', eds A. Morrison, D. Fraiser and J. Kiras, *Peacekeeping with Muscle: The Use of Force in International Conflict Resolution* (Brown Book Co.: Toronto, 1997).

ranging from 'nostalgic images, to management strategies, to visions of communities strong enough to police themselves'.[8] It can refer to a 'contrast to rapid response and enforcement-oriented policing . . . a process by which crime control is shared with the public . . . a means of developing communication with the public and interest groups'.[9] It is not an easy concept to capture and is often contained in eight or 10 principles.[10] This compounds the problems of implementation.

Community policing in essence, and as the term is used in this chapter, proposes a partnership with civil society so that communities can have input into policing and, in return, participate and give support.[11] It is a philosophy which permeates the police department. Importantly, foot patrols and neighbourhood watch schemes are tools of community policing, but a police force can follow community policing without using foot patrols, or have foot patrols without being a community police force.[12]

Community policing has come to be accepted as a positive way of policing society, especially by policy makers and senior police in Western societies, and has become very popular. Different models of community policing are found in Western, Asian and other societies, some focusing on city areas, others on more rural areas. There are, nevertheless, sceptical voices which maintain that it is not necessarily as effective or positive as is claimed.[13] It has been argued that it might not empower communities but on the contrary 'become a device for instructing the populace rather than for listening to it'.[14]

Research has come to different conclusions from city to city and country to country as to the outcome of implementing community policing, and in which cases it is more effective.[15] Moreover, officers' attitudes towards community policing and its effects differ substan-

---

[8] Lyons, W., *The Politics of Community Policing: Rearranging the Power to Punish* (University of Michigan Press: Ann Arbor, Mich., 1999), p. 40.

[9] Fielding, N., *Community Policing* (Clarendon Press: Oxford, 1995), p. 25.

[10] Friedmann (note 3), p. 3. Friedmann also discusses the elusiveness of the concept.

[11] Trojanowicz and Bucqueroux (note 4), p. ix. On the 10 principles of community policing see also pp. xiii–xv.

[12] Bayley (note 5), p. 7.

[13] Fielding (note 9), p. 1; and Manning, P. K. and Singh, M. P., 'Violence and hyperviolence: the rhetoric and practice of community policing', *Sociological Spectrum*, vol. 17, no. 3 (July/Sep. 1997), p. 339.

[14] Bayley, D., 'The contemporary practices of policing: a comparative view', in *Civilian Police and Multinational Peacekeeping* (National Institute of Justice: Washington, DC, 1997), p. 5.

[15] See, e.g., Rosenbaum (note 5) for case study reports.

tially, and they are often ambivalent as to its positive effects.[16] This can partly be explained by the different perspectives on community policing, in addition to the differences between the communities in which it is implemented. If a police force is to employ community policing, the whole force needs to have a clear and consistent understanding of the concept and of how to implement it in the day-to-day maintenance of law and order. This can be highly problematic in national police forces but is worse in international forces, which are mandated to maintain law and order in an alien environment.

In East Timor at one stage 41 different nations were to apply the concept in an international context.

III. Community policing in East Timor

The mission statement for the UN civilian police in East Timor stated:

Respecting the culture of the people, the Mission of UNTAET [the UN Transitional Administration in East Timor] CIVPOL shall be to provide a professional, modern, democratic and *community based* police service to the people of East Timor, to ensure international human rights are protected, and to provide training, guidance and direction in the development of a national police service which shall prevail following the departure of UNTAET.[17]

The reasons for including the concept of community policing in the mission statement do not seem to have been based on a thorough analysis of the potential advantages or limitations of such a policy. The decision to include it seems to have been reached not through careful deliberation of the potential benefits but because of the popularity the concept has in certain circles and because some proponents of community policing have found it beneficial in solving problems in their own home countries. That it might not be applicable in an international context does not seem to have been a major issue.

---

[16] See, e.g., Lurigio, A. and Skogan, W., 'Winning the hearts and minds of police officers: an assessment of staff perceptions of community policing in Chicago', *Crime and Delinquency*, vol. 40, no. 3 (July 1994); Pate, A. and Shtull, P., 'Community policing grows in Brooklyn: an inside view of the New York City Police Department's Model Precinct', *Crime and Delinquency*, vol. 40, no. 3 (July 1994); and Wilson, D. and Bennett, S., 'Officers' response to community policing: variations on a theme', *Crime and Delinquency*, vol. 40, no. 3 (July 1994).

[17] 'UNTAET CivPol administration and operations manual' (note 1), p. 2. Emphasis added.

There were several obstacles facing the CivPols in conducting community policing in East Timor. It was hampered in four main ways. First, there was a lack of definitional clarity: the officers did not know what it entailed. Second, there were no policies for implementation. Third, not all officers were convinced that it was overall a positive concept to apply. Fourth, time and resources were limited. The officers thought that it would take a long time to create a system of community policing and that it would not happen while they where there, hence few made an effort to create any system of community policing.[18] In Dili there were no attempts to implement any form of community policing. The international police were only dealing with day-to-day matters of maintaining law and order. Community policing was not a priority.

With a concept as elusive as community policing and without sharply defined guidelines, the result of 'following community policing' can only be, and was in East Timor, mixed at best. Some examples will serve to illustrate this point.

One deputy commander in a district stated that community policing was followed by CivPols in his district with great success and that they were also teaching the East Timorese Police Service (ETPS) to use it. His core argument about community policing was that CivPols had to 'teach them [the local population] to help themselves'.[19] It was based on the idea that the police should not intervene constantly, but rather remain in their offices and only venture out when it was very important. He saw community policing as a way to end extensive police involvement in the community and as an opportunity for the communities to police themselves.[20] In other districts CivPol officers defined community policing as building volleyball and basketball courts and arranging matches between themselves or international staff and the local population.[21] One senior CivPol officer's definition was 'problem solving through consultation'.[22] On the basis of their own interpretations of what community policing consisted of, CivPol officers in the different districts of East Timor sometimes argued that a high degree of community policing existed, and that the mandate

[18] Author's interview with CivPol officers in Dili and the districts.
[19] Author's interview with a CivPol district deputy commander, 29 Mar. 2001.
[20] Author's interview with a CivPol district deputy commander, 29 Mar. 2001.
[21] Author's interviews with CivPol district deputy commanders, Apr. 2001.
[22] Author's interviews with a senior CivPol officer in Dili, 3 Apr. 2001.

was being carried out according to community policing principles, while other officers in the same districts, who had a different definition of community policing, felt that it had been completely abandoned.[23]

Many officers could not define community policing at all and had a very unclear idea what the concept meant. On one level some officers haphazardly followed community policing in some areas. Some of the tools of community policing were sometimes applied, but it was far from being a philosophy throughout a police department or indeed a partnership with the community. There was no structure to the application of the tools of community policing and no coherent policy. A few districts had a community CivPol police officer, but not all. It is not evident what difference having such an officer made. The *Community Policing Weekly Reports* issued by some districts mention vehicle and foot patrols, informal lectures to schools, recruitment and training of the ETPS, reported crimes and community activities,[24] which underlines the wide range of what was considered to be community policing.

Concern was voiced from some quarters over the potential impact of community policing. Human rights officers argued that it could be interpreted as community spying.[25] This was mentioned in relation to such things as neighbourhood watch schemes. During the Indonesian occupation, systems were put in place to keep the local population under control. Indonesian forces were seriously abusive, and hence distrusted; consequently, alternative methods of dealing with crime and its perpetrators were used increasingly during the occupation. This resulted in an extensive resort to traditional methods of justice— one of the factors which significantly complicate the use of community policing by international forces.

This is a potential difficulty in any post-conflict society. Abusive security forces entice the local population to take part in 'security', particularly as informants. This type of policing can therefore conjure up negative memories. There are potential problems with introducing schemes that reflect or remind the local population of such previous security arrangements. Models of policing which include close cooperation with security forces (from different nationalities, more-

---

[23] Author's interviews with CivPol officers in the districts, Mar.–Apr. 2001.

[24] UNTAET, *Community Policing Weekly Reports*, various issues.

[25] Author's interviews with human rights officers in Dili and districts, Mar.–Apr. 2001.

over) will therefore ultimately be difficult, if not impossible, to follow, particularly without a parallel process of education of the civilian population. This must be taken into consideration when deciding whether or not to include community policing in international policing missions.

However, the perspective of the East Timorese did not seem to reflect this worry.[26] There was no opinion as to the possible positive or negative effects of community policing. The whole concept was as unclear to them as it was to the CivPols. There was only limited communication with the population where community policing was to be implemented and little or no discussion with them as to what it meant. Cooperation with the community is the essence of community policing. If the community does not know or recognize this type of policing it will be hard pressed to succeed.

IV. International community policing: an oxymoron?

A key question that must be addressed is whether it is possible to conduct international law enforcement using the concept of community policing.

The existence of a wide range of definitions of the concept of community policing within an international force can make it very difficult to implement. The absence of coherent strategies, definitions and implementation plans, as in East Timor, will lead to non-implementation in the field. 'Community policing' is a buzz word which has spread rather uncritically into an international peace operations context.

There are other potential problems. First, lack of knowledge of local languages makes it very difficult to follow its principles. Second, trust is fundamental for community policing, and this is difficult to establish, among other factors because of the rapid rotation of the international forces.[27] Third, the international police do not know the society in which the mission is carried out or how it functions. Societies are complex: even the international police officers' home

---

[26] Author's interviews with representatives of East Timorese civil society, Mar.–Apr. 2001.

[27] Research has established that people become upset if their police officers who are conducting community policing are transferred quickly. Grinc, R., 'Angels in marble: problems in stimulating community involvement in community policing', *Crime and Delinquency*, vol. 40, no. 3 (July 1994). This would be exacerbated in an international context.

communities are complicated to understand, let alone communities with a culture alien to them. Cultural sensitivity is necessary but not sufficient to implement community policing. There are essential divisions within all communities, and in a foreign context these are more difficult to identify, so that reliance on one part of the community can often become pervasive. Fourth, community policing is seen as a philosophy that should guide the whole police department. This is an impossibility in an international context because of the divergent philosophies of the different national police forces. It is questionable whether such a philosophy could ever be created in an environment consisting of 41 nationalities or more. Fifth, in post-conflict societies people are generally fearful of reprisals, and cooperation with the police can be viewed negatively because of the history of abusive security forces.

Evaluations of one tool of community policing—neighbourhood watch—have shown that it is more successful in homogeneous, affluent middle-class communities.[28] Research has established that the sections of the population that are most in need of police services are less likely to reap any benefits from community policing.[29] This raises the question of how it can be successfully transferred to a post-conflict context.

Community policing entails a partnership between the police and the local communities. For such a partnership to function there must be trust, transparency (which in peace operations must include education) and, more importantly, accountability.

First, building trust is essential, but there is significant mistrust of police and security forces in many countries and in local communities which have known 'democratic policing' for years.[30] This sometimes deep-seated mistrust of law enforcement is often prevalent in communities that experience high levels of police intervention and misconduct. These are often the communities that would benefit the most from developing a partnership with the police and where com-

[28] Bayley, D., 'Community policing: a report from the devil's advocate', eds Greene and Mastrofski (note 3), p. 233.

[29] Rosenbaum, D. and Lurigio, A., 'An inside look at community policing reform: definitions, organisational changes and evaluation findings', *Crime and Delinquency*, vol. 40, no. 3 (July 1994), p. 299.

[30] The term 'democratic policing' is in itself somewhat of a contested concept. In this context, however, it indicated civilian policing providing a service to the population (not protecting the government), while respecting human rights principles.

munity policing would be very beneficial. In conflict or post-conflict societies, such as East Timor, which have experienced prolonged abuse from police and security forces, the trust which is necessary if community policing is to have any meaning will take a long time to build. It is doubtful whether international police in the short space of time for which they are present can overcome the mistrust that is inherent in a post-conflict society, or one still in conflict, and create the necessary level of trust in law enforcement to follow a policy of community policing. When deploying international policing missions there must be an awareness of this issue and they must act to break down these barriers. Instead new barriers are created because of the organization of missions—for instance, lack of language skills and/or interpreters, an inability to explain their role to the local population, insufficient knowledge of the culture and history of the country and the diverse ways in which the law is applied (as was seen in East Timor).

Second, transparency and education are key issues when attempting to carry out community policing. However, police departments are often very closed institutions, protective and to some extent secretive. They tend not to divulge much information. This is also the case in international police operations, as was witnessed in East Timor. The East Timorese indicated dissatisfaction with the amount of information received from the CivPols.[31] There was limited information available to civil society about CivPols and their role, and uncertainty regarding their objectives and mission. Civil society perceived a lack of transparency.[32] They wanted information, but it was not forthcoming.

International police forces must explain their mission, objectives and actions to civil society. There is a tendency in peace operations not to focus on the distribution of information, outreach or education about the role of the police. International police in peace operations must conduct information campaigns explaining their role in the mission country in order to establish trust and to teach the population about the new type of policing. Failure to educate can lead to a negative image of the police and will create barriers to community policing (or in some cases any type of policing). It will hinder the building

---

[31] Author's interviews with representatives of East Timorese civil society in Dili and the districts, Mar.–Apr. 2001.

[32] Author's interviews with representatives of East Timorese NGOs, Dili, Mar.–Apr. 2001.

of partnership between the international police and the local communities. There needs to be communication and interaction at all levels.

In Western countries police departments have discovered that public awareness and education are crucial for community policing.[33] As one observer has stated: 'Any potential for success of community policing will be limited if major commitments to community education and training are not made'.[34] In most peace operations these commitments are not made. However, community policing in a post-conflict context will be impossible if civil society does not know what it entails. The cooperation between the police force and civil society which is necessary for successful implementation of community policing cannot exist without education of the population.

Public awareness and education, however, are not sufficient in themselves. In addition substantial outreach efforts by the police are necessary, including contact with community leaders which demonstrate that the police want to improve the community over a period of time.[35] Such efforts are often close to non-existent in international policing of post-conflict societies and are rarely prioritized.

The third significant problem that will hinder the progress of community policing in an international context is that of accountability. It is questionable whether local communities will be willing to trust and enter into a partnership with law enforcers who cannot be held accountable to local laws, or in many cases are not seen to be accountable at all. The law enforcers often have near-immunity from the laws of the mission country,[36] which sends a negative signal to civil society and lessens the effect of implementing and teaching democratic policing. Making international police forces accountable for their actions during policing missions is particularly important when the mandate includes maintaining law and order.

In East Timor, as in most missions, the CivPol officers were not subject to local laws. This immunity of international law enforcers could lead to a lack of credibility and will reduce the possibilities of cooperation with and from civil society. A police force entrusted with establishing democratic policing should not be above the laws it is

---

[33] Rosenbaum and Lurigio (note 29), p. 299.
[34] Grinc (note 27), p. 14.
[35] Grinc (note 27), p. 14.
[36] See chapter 2, section IV, in this volume.

enforcing. This not only contradicts democratic policing principles, but can also reinforce the negative image of security forces in a society which has had prolonged experience of police and military forces acting above the law. Many CivPol officers in peace operations come from forces which are abusive and in some instances corrupt. If they in any way conduct themselves in a similar manner in the mission country they must be dealt with swiftly. The rules that guide their behaviour should not be separate from those that apply to the local population if they commit crimes against the local population.

The maximum penalty for a serious offence in East Timor, including assault and sexual assault, was repatriation. Again, this could significantly reduce the possibility of the local communities entering into a partnership with the international police force, because civil society would see a police officer committing a crime against a local inhabitant, but the 'punishment' would be a return ticket home. The offending officer could be tried for his offences upon his return home, but it is entirely up to the national government to pursue the case and, more importantly, the local population will never hear of the outcome. To establish trust and partnership, essential for community policing, a structure of accountability is necessary, and this structure is currently non-existent in international policing missions.

Other factors also reduce the potential for the success of community policing. They include resources: community policing needs extensive resources, but international policing operations are always short of resources. More often than not they are forced to make do with what they have. There are also the problems of skills, willingness, short periods of service and absence of knowledge of local communities. These factors further complicate community policing.

It is possible for international forces to use certain tools of community policing, but community policing as a partnership with the population or as a philosophy throughout the CivPol police department is close to impossible. The force can use, for example, foot patrols to get closer to the community and other tools to enhance communication, information and education, but this is not necessarily community policing; as mentioned above, a force can use certain community policing tools without being a community policing force. It would be more useful to get away from the label, and simply implement strategies that can bring civil society and international police closer together. The emphasis must be on education, information and creating awareness about the role of the international police, what civilian policing entails and what can be expected from this different type of policing.

V. Teaching community policing

Teaching community policing as part of police reform in policing missions is an easier task. It is less complicated to teach the tools of community policing to a homogeneous local police force than for a multinational police force to implement it in a foreign context and culture. However, the methods and structures for doing so must be in place. A policy of teaching community policing (and what type of community policing model should be applied) must be established before deployment and the decision as to the type of community policing model to be established must be taken in consultation with local leaders, so that they do not simply receive a model they cannot relate to. 'Ownership' of this process is key.

In East Timor the civilian police decided that the Koban model of community policing was to be implemented.[37] It was chosen because it is an Asian model—originally Japanese, with elements from Singapore incorporated—and there was an assumption that it would fit the existing socio-political structure in East Timor. However, the decision to apply this model was not reached through extensive consultation with local leaders. In addition, the model was never really explained to the CivPols or to the local police force.

Teaching community policing also encounters the same problems as training a new local police force in general—culture, language, short-term commitment, lack of resources and lack of knowledge of the society. In addition, two particular problems stand out.

First, many officers who are providing the instruction do not deal with community policing in their home countries and can hardly be expected to teach something they do not know if they have not been trained in it. Second, many officers do not believe it to be a solution to the problems of crime. They might therefore not be particularly inclined to emphasize and teach the tools of community policing or its

---

[37] The main features of the Koban system include police posts in residential areas, 24-hour operation, police responsibility for peace and security, and a base for police activities in cooperation with the community. Pomerville, P. and Wairoa-Harrison, W., 'Feasibility study for community policing based on the KOBAN system', UNTAET CivPol headquarters, 13 Sep. 2000, p. 11.

philosophy. A solution to this would be to train key international police officers to deal specifically with the teaching of community policing to the local forces. A coherent policy of community policing could then be taught to the new force. Yet, again, there must also be a parallel process of education and information to the civil population explaining what this type of policing entails, what it means for them and how it can benefit the community.

The value of teaching community policing in a particular country must be assessed, rather than uncritically assuming that it is the best solution. If it is decided that it should be applied, this should be incorporated in the training given prior to arrival in the mission area. It is essential that it should not be up to each commander, or in some instances each individual international police officer, to define and interpret what community policing is and then decide whether or not it is worth teaching.

In East Timor the induction course given by the UN prior to deployment included a section on community policing.[38] However, it consisted of 17 slides in a PowerPoint presentation (in contrast, there were 26 slides on the history of the UN). If the international community is to incorporate community policing into peace operations, much more extensive training is required, both of the international officers and of civil society. Otherwise it becomes nothing more than paying lip-service to a buzz word.

VI. Conclusions

1. The fact that people are questioning the value of community policing in national policing should be considered when arguing for its use by an international police force with a law enforcement mandate. Evaluation of community policing programmes is difficult because they are seldom implemented as planned.[39] If opinion is divided as to whether they work in national police forces, an even more cautious and critical approach is necessary when promoting community policing in an international context. The problems that face national police forces implementing community policing can only be exacerbated in an international context.

[38] UN Transitional Administration in East Timor, Induction Training Unit, 'Induction training handbook', Nov. 2000, pp. 65–67.
[39] Rosenbaum and Lurigio (note 29), p. 299.

2. The elusive nature of the concept of community policing under-lines the need for a clear definition and implementation plans if it is to be applied in peace operations. No UN document that referred to the use of community policing in East Timor defined the concept or explained it in depth.

3. Certain conditions must be met for an international force to police a country following the principles of community policing: (*a*) an assessment establishing it as the best solution for the territory; (*b*) the construction of a policy framework, a definition and implementation plans; (*c*) pre-deployment training of international police officers; (*d*) an information and education campaign for civil society; (*e*) a higher level of transparency than presently exists; and (*f*) revised accountability structures.

4. These are necessary but not sufficient conditions for an inter-national police force to implement a policy of community policing. The establishment of a bond between the international police and civil society is crucial in a post-conflict society, but using community policing by international law enforcers to establish this link is very difficult. Community policing is too complex and resource-demanding and involves too many difficulties to be applied by an international force. Instead of using such a large concept as community policing, emphasis should be placed on simpler strategies to enhance closer cooperation with the population which must be rooted in communica-tion and education.

5. It would be more beneficial to focus on teaching community policing to local forces than to insist on international forces using it when enforcing law and order. Community policing should not be included in international policing missions merely because of the popularity of the concept.

5. Civil–military cooperation: the military, paramilitaries and civilian police in executive policing

Annika S. Hansen

I. Introduction

Civil–military cooperation is nothing new and has been a standard part of peace operations at least since the early 1990s.[1] With the expansion of peace operations in the course of the past decade, the term 'civil–military cooperation' has come to incorporate a wide range of efforts to secure cooperation and coordination between the activities of civilian agencies and those of the military forces in a conflict area. At the same time, law-and-order issues have come to the fore as a central concern in any peace operation. This has brought the relationship between military forces and the international civilian police (CivPols) into the spotlight, as public security is the realm in which the paths of the military and the civilian police, as the relevant key players in the civilian reconstruction effort, cross most frequently.

In the civilian police monitoring operations of the early 1990s, military–police cooperation was limited and consisted mainly of logistical support.[2] However, with the steadily expanding role of civilian police in peace operations, the interface between military and police staff has increased, providing more opportunities and placing greater demands on cooperation between the two.

Concerns over cooperation have been heightened in the light of the most recent development towards executive policing, where international security actors assume full responsibility for law enforcement, and which effectively places the military forces and their civilian police counterparts in the same boat. In these situations it is to

---

[1] The term civil–military relations as it is used in the present context differs from—but is sometimes confused with—the military term, CIMIC. In military terminology, CIMIC refers to a specific arrangement by which civilian experts such as engineers and lawyers are deployed with a military force.

[2] Examples are the UN operations in Namibia (the UN Transitional Assistance Group, UNTAG, 1989–90) and Angola (the UN Angola Verification Missions, UNAVEM I and II, 1988–95).

all international security forces—military and police—that the population of a war-torn society turn for a tangible improvement in their personal safety. In the two executive policing missions that have been initiated so far, in Kosovo and East Timor, it proved extremely difficult to establish public security. The shortcomings of the police and the military contingent indicated that neither was able to fill the public security 'gap' on its own and that effective executive policing depended on improving the patchy cooperation between the two.

Examples of current military–police cooperation are (in addition to continued logistical support) joint patrolling, military back-up, temporary use of military facilities for law enforcement purposes, such as for detention centres, and cooperation on criminal investigations.

In an attempt to address the gaps in military–police cooperation and deal with the 'grey-area' challenges that lay between peacekeeping and policing, decision makers introduced designated specialized and 'formed' police units, which they believed would be the perfect hybrid. Although the role of formed police units, also called 'police with military status' or 'gendarmerie-type forces', is difficult to assess, there can be no doubt that they now play a part in civil–military cooperation.

While there is some cause for optimism and there are clear windows of opportunity in civil–military cooperation, the recent expansion of cooperation also points to the complexity and the limitations of military involvement in policing. In particular, the culture and organization of the military and those of the police and the links between the two differ widely in different contributing countries, not to mention diverging national interests, domestic policies and budget constraints.[3] This makes generalizations on the ability and suitability of the military in policing difficult, although some fundamental and conceptual issues are the same in all peace operations.

This chapter discusses the relations and divisions of labour between different actors involved in the specific context of executive policing. Most of the evidence is therefore drawn from the peace operations in Kosovo and East Timor, but there are references also to the cases of Haiti, Somalia and Cambodia. The evidence shows that there is a recognition among the military and the police that close and more effective cooperation is pivotal and that there is a willingness to

---

[3] Hills, A., 'The inherent limits of military forces in policing peace operations', *International Peacekeeping*, vol. 8, no. 3 (autumn 2001), pp. 86–91.

improve existing cooperation patterns. However, a number of problems remain and have the potential to be crippling unless resolved. Among these are: finding effective modes of cooperation at a tactical level; overcoming the organizational and cultural differences between the military and the civilian police in order to enable real joint planning; and developing a chain of command that is effective, flexible and acceptable to both the military and the civilian police forces.

II. The evolving military–police relationship

A thin line between love and hate

The debate on the division of labour between the military and police officers is one that has recurred throughout the history of CivPol contributions to peacekeeping and has been heated at times.

Some of the effects of the shortcomings the civilian police grapple with, including delays in deployment, the recruitment of sufficient (and adequate) staff and resource shortages, can be mitigated by better cooperation with military. Again, these shortfalls have greater implications in an executive policing operation in which the international police assume full responsibility for law and order, and they undermine the credibility of the civilian police. José Ramos Horta, Special Representative of the National Council of Maubere Resistance of East Timor and a Nobel Peace Prize winner, had little faith in some of the CivPol staff he encountered in East Timor and even described the deployment of unqualified policemen as 'insulting'.[4]

Not only have peace operations become more intrusive in recent years; they are also undertaken in more unstable and criminalized conditions. In these conditions the civilian police, who never have and do not aspire to have full area control, can benefit hugely from military support as a force multiplier. In a war-torn society, where 'might' often still equals 'right', military back-up provides civilian police with a much-needed credibility boost.

However, while cooperation with the military has made the efforts of civilian police in peace operations more effective than in the past, there is a danger of assuming that it can provide all the answers to the conceptual and operational challenges of civilian police deployment.

---

[4] Traub, J., 'Inventing East Timor', *Foreign Affairs*, vol. 79, no. 4 (July/Aug. 2000), p. 85.

Moreover, the debate seized on civilian police as a welcome alternative to military forces in the late 1990s. In part, the deployment of police was promoted because they were the cheaper and lower-profile option for contributing governments.[5] With the emergence of public security issues as the key to stabilizing a war-torn society and to consolidating a peace process, there was a tendency to put an increasing share of the responsibility for restoring and maintaining security onto the shoulders of civilian police. This suited the military, who had never been keen to take on policing tasks. The instinctive rejection of policing tasks by the military disregarded the fact that forces had 'done' policing in the past with military police and similar force units. On the part of the United States, the reluctance of the military to engage in policing was reinforced by the experiences in Somalia—ironically, since the limited assistance the Unified Task Force (UNITAF) gave to the indigenous police force was one of the more successful aspects of the international intervention in Somalia.

With the operations in Kosovo and East Timor, attitudes among North American and European military staff have shifted slightly and there is a greater openness towards revising the division of labour. This move appears to be driven more by the rank and file than by their political masters. To some extent the military have overcome their reluctance to be engaged in policing because to restore self-sustaining public security is increasingly seen as an effective, and perhaps the only viable, 'exit strategy'. This was stated as early as in the military approach to operations in Haiti and Somalia, and was gradually understood by the commanders of the Stabilization Force (SFOR) in Bosnia and Herzegovina and the Kosovo Force (KFOR).[6] However, there is also a danger of the opposite extreme if military forces in their new-found eagerness assume policing tasks that they are not qualified for and thereby undermine the fledgling rule of law. Clearly, it is imperative to take a closer look at the limitations and pitfalls of military–police cooperation in order to develop a differentiated and cohesive approach.

---

[5] They are not cheaper per person, but governments can, e.g., second a handful of policemen while an equivalent military contribution might be some hundreds of soldiers.

[6] On Haiti see Bailey, M. *et al.,* 'Haiti: military–police partnership for public security', eds R. B. Oakley, M. J. Dziedzic and E. M. Goldberg, *Policing the New World Disorder* (National Defense University Press: Washington, DC, 1998), p. 251. On Somalia see Thomas, L. and Spataro, S., 'Peacekeeping and policing in Somalia', *Policing the New World Disorder*, pp. 187, 205, 212.

The introduction of paramilitary units

Recently the debate on the extent of military involvement in law and order has also encompassed police with military status. The use of security forces whose roles fall somewhere in between that of the military and that of the police is not new, but experiences with formed police units have been mixed and their role has evolved greatly over the course of the 1990s. In 2001 observers were increasingly hailing police with military status as the panacea for many of the internal security issues that arise in the wake of conflicts. The role of formed police units has to be factored in to considerations of chain of command and the potential for developing working relationships between the military and the civilian police forces.

The empirical basis for evaluating formed police units is limited: assessments of their role tend to be anecdotal and tied to specific cases. They are also difficult to assess because their usefulness, effectiveness and credibility vary greatly with the nationality of each contingent. There is no such thing as a standard 'gendarmerie-type' force: they are trained, structured and deployed differently in accordance with domestic security needs in the home country. Formed police units have the potential to play an important role, but several problematic issues have emerged from their deployment to date that should temper the optimism about their usefulness.

Early deployments took place in 1992–95, when contingents from the Spanish Guardia Civil and the Argentinian Gendarmeria Nacional were deployed in Haiti and El Salvador, respectively. In Haiti, the US Military Police and special forces worked closely with civilian police and the Haitian National Police on joint patrols and provided communication support at police stations.[7] In contrast to later deployments, these formed police units were integrated into the international police or military force without separately defined functions.

By the late 1990s, formed police units were regarded as a strategic asset specifically designed to fill a perceived gap between military capabilities and the abilities of unarmed police monitors. A Multinational Specialized Unit (MSU) was created for this purpose for the first time under SFOR in 1998.[8] The MSU was charged with the

---

[7] Two hundred US and 120 Indian military police stayed on under US command during the subsequent UN Mission in Haiti (UNMIH). Bailey *et al*. (note 6), pp. 227ff, 233.

[8] The MSU consisted of 350 Italian *carabinieri* and minor contributions of Argentinian Gendarmeria Nacional, Romanian Politia Militari and Slovenian Military Police.

protection of returnees and elected officials, and could be called on to assist in preserving public order at the request of the International Police Task Force (IPTF). It patrols regularly, but by 2001 had, according to one MSU commander, 'only actually twice . . . intervene[d] in troubles'.[9] Still, experiences in Bosnia and Herzegovina were deemed satisfactory enough to convince decision makers that an MSU in Kosovo would be essential to success.

In this way, police with military status have come to be regarded as an essential force component in executive policing. Indeed, planners in Kosovo created an MSU under KFOR command *and* a Special Police Unit (SPU), which is part of the UN Interim Administration Mission in Kosovo (UNMIK) Police and has a remit similar to that of the MSU.[10] The UN civilian police in East Timor also featured a gendarmerie element, called the Rapid Response Unit, which consisted of 120 Portuguese and 120 Jordanian police with military status to deal with major security threats and large-scale emergencies.

Paramilitary units appear to have come to stay. Like military–police cooperation more generally, they offer potential, but also add to the complexity of the challenges, for example, of using muscular back-up wisely and of ensuring continuity and consistency throughout the law enforcement effort. They also face much the same problems as military and police forces in peace operations—their multinational composition, unclear mandates and the difficulty of meeting recruitment demands.

III. Gaps to be filled and challenges to be met

In order to better grasp why military–police cooperation is pivotal in executive policing and where its potential lies, it is helpful to take a closer look at the gaps that cooperation is intended to fill. Alice Hills, lecturer at the British Joint Services Command and Staff College,

---

[9] MSU commander quoted in Barber, L. (Capt.), 'MSU, the SFOR force multiplier', *SFOR Informer*, no. 92 (19 July 2000), available at URL <http://www.nato.int/sfor/indexinf/92/msufor/t000719l.htm>. The IPTF is a component of the UN Mission in Bosnia and Herzegovina (UNMIBH), 1995 to date.

[10] The primary tasks of the MSU are law enforcement, in particular criminal intelligence on organized crime, and the handling of civil disturbances. The SPU in Kosovo was intended to contribute to the protection of UN staff, to provide operational support and back-up to civilian police, to deal with threats to public order in coordination with KFOR and to assist the nascent Kosovo Police Service with crowd control. United Nations, Department of Peacekeeping Operations, Civilian Police Division, 'Guidelines for governments contributing special police units to UNMIK', 1999, p. 9.

suggests that there are two main gaps in the provision of a secure and stable environment—a deployment and an enforcement gap.[11]

The deployment gap

The notion of a deployment gap originates in a discussion of military–police cooperation that regards an operation as a series of phases.[12] There are important differences in the issues that are dominant in the different phases: for instance, planning is especially critical early on and, as a general rule, the military force will have a greater role in early stages because it takes longer to deploy police and levels of instability are higher in the immediate post-conflict phase. The need for coordination between the military and the police is arguably greatest in the pre-deployment and initial deployment phases. At this stage provisions can be made to address challenges such as the inevitable time lag between mission initiation and deployment of the full police contingent. In an executive policing mission, the international forces present are expected to enforce the law from 'day one', at which time the CivPol contingent is never in place.[13] Moreover, in the early days of a mission the situation is often so volatile that a convincing case can be made for the military force, being the more capable and the available actor, to maintain order at this stage.

Before the long-term efforts to build the institutions of the local judicial system have gathered momentum, the military task of providing a secure environment coincides to a great extent with the demand for public security. The military can alleviate public security concerns at the outset of an operation by providing equipment and other logistics support, by offering military facilities, as well as military lawyers, by conducting increased patrols and so on.[14] While underlining the value of military support to law enforcement, Hansjoerg Strohmeyer, legal adviser in both Kosovo and East Timor, also emphasizes that the role must be a stopgap only, to be terminated as soon as sufficient civilian capacity, including civilian police,

[11] Hills (note 3), pp. 80–82.

[12] See, e.g., chapter 3 in this volume.

[13] Strohmeyer argues this point for both Kosovo and East Timor. Strohmeyer, H., 'Collapse and reconstruction of a judicial system: the United Nations missions in Kosovo and East Timor', *American Journal of International Law*, vol. 95, no. 1 (Jan. 2001), p. 60.

[14] Both KFOR in Kosovo and the International Force for East Timor (INTERFET) in East Timor arrested and detained a significant number of suspects when the UN civilian police and justice components were unable to do so. Strohmeyer (note 13), pp. 51, 57–58, 61.

civilian judges and prison staff, is in place.[15] At a political level, the establishment phase is the time when a cohesive approach to the overarching goals of an operation should be developed among and communicated to the major contributors, and particularly the military and the civilian police.

However, once an operation is under way the analysis of cooperation would benefit from a more differentiated approach, as levels of violence and thus the need for more military support vary from day to day and from region to region. The approach has to build on a detailed understanding of various individual police functions within an executive policing mandate, as outlined in chapter 3.

The deployment gap may include shortfalls in the numbers of staff throughout the course of the mission. Here military forces can provide invaluable relief to civilian police forces and contribute to maintaining law and order even once the CivPol contingent has been deployed and the operation is under way. For example, military patrols in the conflict area increase the visibility and credibility of the usually thinly-stretched civilian police. Haiti is one example of earlier peacekeeping operations—with traits of executive policing—in which military and police cooperated closely and effectively. Joint patrols in Haiti were nicknamed 'four men in a jeep' and included an international and a local policeman, a military peacekeeper and an interpreter.[16]

Formed police units have been hailed as a way to get forces on the ground quickly. However, they are as difficult to recruit as civilian police since they, too, usually form part of the daily public security structures in their home countries. They therefore cannot necessarily help in filling the deployment gap. Italy is perhaps the exception, with its massive and intricate network of security forces, 120 000 of which are *carabinieri*—gendarmes. The recruitment difficulty is diminishing slightly as more potential contributors are made aware of the need for formed police units in peace operations and are coming forward with various kinds of police with military status. For many countries, reclassifying security forces is a convenient way of filling their quotas of civilian police for peace operations in one fell swoop while avoiding taking police officers off their own domestic beat. Some of the offers of troops pose further problems: as with civilian police, a

[15] Strohmeyer (note 13), p. 61.

[16] In Bosnia and Herzegovina the effectiveness of the IPTF was greatly enhanced when joint patrols with the Stabilization Force (SFOR) were introduced in 1997.

number of these forces come from countries in which democratic standards are not upheld.

Crowd control is one of the most central tasks for formed police units in the executive policing missions in Kosovo and East Timor. Here formed police units play a more confrontational role than civilian police. Arguably, paramilitaries with non-democratic backgrounds are a problem for formed police units and can have a greater destabilizing effect.

The enforcement gap

The second and more difficult gap to bridge is the enforcement gap. Where the moral authority of the civilian police is not sufficient to enforce the law, military forces can contribute muscular back-up, engage in counter-terrorism work or help in crowd control. Mandates now commonly call on the military to 'provide a secure environment'—both for the international civilian staff and for the local population. In Haiti, the Multi-national Force (MNF) was specially designed to create the stable conditions necessary for the deployment of the UN Mission in Haiti (UNMIH) which then took over in the spring of 1995. The 300 unarmed monitors of the UN Mission in East Timor (UNAMET) were helpless in the face of the growing violence there. The Australian-led military International Force for East Timor (INTERFET) restored order and arguably set a more forceful tone for the deployment of UNTAET.[17]

Both cases point to another important aspect of cooperation between military and police—the question whether the military have an enforcement mandate and are authorized to 'use all necessary means', as INTERFET was in East Timor, the MNF was in Haiti and the UN Mission in Somalia (UNOSOM II) was in Somalia.

The security situation in Kosovo and the assumption of executive authority by NATO and the UN even forced the UN Security Council to include 'ensuring public safety and order' in KFOR's mandate 'until the international civil presence can take responsibility for this task'.[18] However, when the military act as a force multiplier for the police, the benefit of the deterrent effect that the military undoubtedly have is not clear-cut. The civilian police gain in credibility by being

---

[17] Strohmeyer (note 13), pp. 51, 54; and Traub (note 4), pp. 77ff.
[18] UN Security Council Resolution 1244, 10 June 1999, para. 9(d), reproduced in appendix A in this volume.

able to call on a coercive threat—military back-up—but the close association with a military force can also undermine public confidence and trust in a newly established or reformed rule of law. This is especially true in countries where the military have been the occupying forces of a 'foreign power', as in Kosovo and East Timor, or an instrument of oppression and of domestic politics, as in El Salvador or Haiti.

In practice, the tendency to lump constituent tasks into two large piles, one labelled 'military' and the other labelled 'police', has proved unhelpful. The key in military–police relations is to develop a better understanding of what exactly enforcing law and order in a foreign and war-torn country entails. It will be critical to arrive at a sophisticated and flexible distribution of labour in complex police operations. The cooperation that emerged in Cambodia is a good example. There the military–police distinction was hazy—for instance, UN CivPols provided a security presence at the polling stations while military peacekeepers secured the approaches to the polling stations.[19] Experience from East Timor also highlights how problematic the division of labour can be. While CivPols were expected to protect minorities, among them returning refugees, some of whom were suspected militia members, the military peacekeepers were called on to 'respond robustly'[20] to threats from the very same Indonesian militias. It is not difficult to see how potentially conflicting tasks can introduce friction into military–police cooperation.

Moreover, working together at a tactical level has clear limitations which spring from the different organizational structures and professional cultures of the military and the police. A policeman is used to acting, and authorized to act, as an individual, making decisions based on his own discretion and personal assessment of a given situation; most soldiers are not, which may inhibit their ability to respond effectively.[21] The military are composed of self-contained units; the

[19] Lee Kim, C. M. and Metrikas, M., 'Holding a fragile peace: the military and civilian components of UNTAC', eds M. W. Doyle, I. Johnstone and R. C. Orr, *Keeping the Peace: Multidimensional UN Operations in Cambodia and El Salvador* (Cambridge University Press: Cambridge, 1997), p. 108.

[20] The term was used by UN Secretary-General Kofi Annan in Sep. 2000 and cited in Human Rights Watch (HRW), *World Report 2001* (HRW: Washington, DC and London, 2001), p. 1, available at URL <http://www.hrw.org/wr2k1/asia/etimor3.html>.

[21] Military police officers are an exception, but generally military forces' concern for the safety of their personnel takes precedence over the potential gains of individual effort and in that way limits flexibility. This is in no way a criticism of military organization, but must be kept in mind when assessing the extent and nature of military–police cooperation.

CivPol component consists of individuals who are dependent on community support for communications, logistics and transport.

The military and the police also differ in their approaches to the use of force, which further complicates the above-mentioned deterrent effect. Hills regards this as the greatest obstacle for military involvement in policing. She points out that the military are the 'coercive resource of last resort' and argues that they cannot be seen to fail, in contrast to the police who rely on discretion and de-escalation of violence.[22] The enforcement gap is vastly complex and can only be filled by developing 'effective functional relationships'. In practice, Hills suggests that these relationships can be fostered by co-locating headquarters, liaison procedures and officers, and by developing compatible contingency plans and standard operating procedures.[23]

The usefulness of the MSU as a more forceful alternative in Bosnia and Herzegovina was initially hampered by the absence of a clear mandate, which prevented its capabilities from being fully exploited.[24] Although some progress has been made, the overlap between MSU and SPU functions in Kosovo indicates that neither NATO nor the UN has thought through what exactly the gap is that formed police units should fill. A better understanding of the strengths and weaknesses of each national contingent is essential to mapping out how formed police units can usefully fill the gap between military and police forces.

It is important to keep in mind that the relationships, as well as the tasks, of the military and the police are complex and that it will be impossible to plan, train and otherwise prepare for all contingencies. It is therefore essential to strengthen mutual awareness and improve communication between the two. The exposure of military officers to civilian police concerns, and vice versa, in Kosovo and East Timor has already brought the military and police forces closer together and is laying a foundation for future cooperation. Regular consultations, such as take place in Kosovo, are an important step towards if not joint, then at least coordinated planning.

Military–police cooperation in practice resembles developments in peace operations more generally, where lessons identified in the field do not filter through to home governments, who are the ones that

---

[22] Hills (note 3), pp. 81, 94.

[23] Hills (note 3), pp. 80ff, 93.

[24] Jane's Information Group, 'The role of police–military units in peace-keeping', available at URL <http://www.janes.com/police/editors/peacekeeping.htm>.

would be able to institutionalize measures for long-term improvements in civil–military cooperation. Practical measures, such as conducting joint exercises or creating the capacity to dispatch key police personnel in advance teams, would be relatively easy to put into place; the real bottleneck is fostering a favourable attitude towards military support to law and order among contributing governments.

Joint planning and the lack of a common language

'Joint planning' is one of the new catchphrases in official documents, such as the UN's Brahimi Report[25] and European Union (EU) documents. While frequency of use does not invalidate it as a key measure that will enhance military–police cooperation, an approach that takes a closer look at what joint planning means and where it fits into military–police cooperation is called for. Joint planning should be reviewed along two main dimensions. First, there is a chronological dimension: pre-mission planning and preparation should be distinguished from ongoing coordination and planning for joint operations or action. Second, joint planning can be established at the level of mission structure and at the level of individual officers and soldiers.

Efforts to enhance cohesion, especially through joint fact-finding and subsequent joint planning in the pre-mission stage, are critical but still face daunting obstacles. Before the large-scale missions of the Balkans and East Timor, civilian police were long considered an 'add-on' and a subordinate activity to peacekeeping, as the case of Mozambique illustrates.[26] Although this view is slowly changing, the legacy of thinking—that planning for an operation is exclusively military—still dominates. This has contributed to delays in the deployment of civilian police and has resulted in poor cooperation between the military and the civilian components in the early stages of a mission.

In the Brahimi Report, specific measures were proposed to involve police officers in the military forces' pre-planning and fact-finding.[27]

[25] United Nations, Report of the Panel on Peacekeeping Operations, UN document A/55/305, S/2000/809, 21 Aug. 2000 (the Brahimi Report).

[26] Little funding was available for CivPols in the UN Mission in Mozambique (ONUMOZ), and an expansion of the mission was only made possible when money was transferred from the military or ceasefire budget. Woods, J. L., 'Mozambique: the CIVPOL operation', *Policing the New World Disorder* (note 6), p. 161.

[27] The Brahimi Report (note 25) emphasizes the need for access to 'standing' and 'standby' resources through 'on-call lists' and 'rosters' (paras 92–101) and the presence of

It is as yet not clear whether or in what form the proposals will be institutionalized. Discussions on mechanisms for joint planning and improved cooperation are also under way in other international organizations which are preparing for the deployment of military and police forces, such as the EU, or which have authorized missions in the past, such as the Organization for Security and Co-operation in Europe (OSCE). In all these discussions, civilian police planners and practitioners have voiced concern about being marginalized if they are integrated into existing military planning processes, as they bring less 'clout' to the table and are in reality less well prepared conceptually.

Joint planning faces another challenge in that it not only involves a clear, defined set of military and police planners but also stretches across several organizations and across different parts of the contributing national authorities. So far it has proved extremely difficult to build meaningful contacts between all the decision makers involved at the national and international levels. Where there has been contact, it has too often been personalized and of an ad hoc nature. This is true of relations between the UN and NATO as well as relations with the EU and the OSCE.

Whether it takes place pre-mission or is ongoing, at headquarters or among policemen and soldiers, planning is plagued by an important deficit: there is no common conceptual or 'doctrinal' basis. Until the publication of the *Principles and Guidelines* for UN civilian police in mid-2001[28] there was very little conceptual thinking on police operations and, while the guidelines indicate an increased awareness among UN planners in New York of the need to formulate a set of principles, they are not comparable to a military doctrine. The lack of dialogue and exchange on a potential doctrine for police missions is in stark contrast to the military tradition in which there are clear distinctions between doctrine, rules of engagement (ROE) and operational planning.

The discrepancy between the military and the police is highly problematic, as it leads to misunderstandings during the planning and implementation of joint operations. When the international military and police forces share operational authority in an executive policing

'military advisors and police experts' in the proposed Information and Strategic Analysis Secretariat (EISAS) (para. 70). It also advocates the creation of an Integrated Mission Task Force (IMTF). Report of the Panel on Peacekeeping Operations (note 25), paras 198–217.

[28] United Nations, Department of Peace-keeping Operations, *United Nations Civilian Police Principles and Guidelines* (UN: New York, 2001).

mission, these misunderstandings can render the law enforcement effort ineffective, for instance, when arrests are botched, evidence is unsuitable for use in court or the protection of threatened individuals breaks down.[29] In an executive policing context, the military and the police are the law: if they are seen as contradictory and inconsistent they lose all credibility and moral authority in the eyes of the local population. In part the lack of mutual conceptual understanding is due to the absence of a common terminology but, more importantly, civilian police activity is marked by a glaring absence of doctrine and the military are guided religiously by their doctrine. The conceptual differences are reflected in and reinforced by different methods of operation, patterns of deployment and organizational structures.

Conceptual differences are also an important issue between police with military status and civilian police, and can lead to inconsistent and ineffective policing. Especially in training local police forces, it is extremely problematic if formed police units and civilian police—who not the least lead by example—conduct two fundamentally different types of executive policing.

This problem was demonstrated, for example, in Kosovo, where the Italian *carabinieri* dominated the MSU and introduced their own brand of policing into the area. Although they proved instrumental in the fight against organized crime, particularly smuggling and human trafficking, they clashed with UNMIK police on ethics and on matters of authority. As in Italy, the *carabinieri* tend to act independently and have been reluctant to submit to the law as it is enforced by the UN, thereby undermining cohesion and the promotion of one rule of law applicable to all.[30] The pattern has been repeated in several cases. In Somalia, the independence of the Italian *carabinieri* and the French gendarmerie undermined police training by introducing paramilitary elements. The same thing happened in Haiti, when the French gendarmerie took over, under the UN Support Mission in Haiti (UNSMIH), from the earlier, more multinational UN effort and the focus of Haitian National Police training shifted away from community policing.[31] Similarly, according to one news report, the Portuguese formed

[29] See also chapter 2, section III, in this volume.

[30] Personal communications at the Civilian Police Division of the UN Department of Peace-keeping Operations, New York, Nov. 2000; and with staff of UNMIK and UNMIBH, London, Mar. 2001, Paris, Mar. 2001, Stockholm, May 2001, Ottawa, June 2001, and Berlin, June 2001.

[31] On Somalia see Thomas and Spataro (note 6), p. 210. On Haiti see Bailey *et al.* (note 6), p. 244.

police unit in East Timor did not prove very skilled at community relations, displaying macho, colonial-type behaviour and earning the description 'gorillas' from the East Timorese.[32]

Military forces are still highly ambivalent about their role in executive policing and doctrinal development in this area is slow. A key issue for further research will be to identify where it is possible to develop common doctrine; where common doctrine is unhelpful, unsuitable, undesirable or damaging; and how, if they cannot coincide, military and police guidelines can be made congruent.

Organizational constellations and chain of command

Civil–military cooperation in executive policing also takes place within different organizational constellations of military and police peace operations. In Cambodia, Eastern Slavonia and, most importantly, East Timor, military–police cooperation took place in a pure UN operation where the CivPol component played a substantial role. In these UN-only cases the lines of authority within a mission were separate: the CivPol commissioner or a chief police officer reported directly to the Special Representative of the UN Secretary-General (SRSG) on a par with the military commanding officer.

In contrast to East Timor, in the police mission in Kosovo responsibility for the executive policing component remained in the hands of the UN,[33] with a military counterpart provided by NATO. The picture may be further complicated in the future when regional and sub-regional organizations—whether the EU, the OSCE or the Economic Community of West African States (ECOWAS)—take over from the UN at a regional level. The EU, for one, has placed the ability to substitute for a local police force—that is, to conduct executive policing—at the top of the list of priorities for its stand-by civilian police capacity.

Practical difficulties can emerge in terms of access to the operation's funding and resources, lines of command and competing authority in an area of operation. Anecdotal evidence is available, but a more detailed comparative analysis of the experiences in Kosovo and East Timor has yet to be conducted. Such a thorough analysis will be critical to understanding to what extent the fact that the civilian police

---

[32] 'Verkauft und verraten' [Sold and betrayed], *Der Spiegel*, 27 Aug. 2001, p. 152.
[33] The OSCE was responsible for training local police and for institutional development.

and the military were both UN-led, as in East Timor, or were not, as in Kosovo, has had a beneficial or detrimental effect on military–police cooperation.

Military and police planners in Kosovo addressed potential problems of competing authority by developing a flexible chain of command which is similar to that established between the former Royal Ulster Constabulary and the British forces in Northern Ireland. Authority moved from the military to the police commander and back in accordance with the level of tension in a given area at a given time.[34] The relationship between the military and the police in Northern Ireland has developed over a long period of time and is reflected in closer contact between the police authorities and the British Ministry of Defence than is common in contributing countries. Military officers from other countries are therefore less likely to submit to the final authority of a police officer in the context of a peace operation.

The question of lines of command also applies to formed police units and the degree of autonomy they enjoy. The MSUs in Kosovo and Bosnia and Herzegovina were under strict military command and had the same ROE as KFOR and SFOR, respectively, but that did not mean that the two acted conformably or cohesively. Although there is value in the flexible response option that the MSU provides in theory, their role in practice is still somewhat unpredictable. In Kosovo, for example, their usefulness depended on how well the different unit commanders got along with their regional counterparts in KFOR. Hills summarizes the ambiguity that accompanies the deployment of MSUs:

Gendarmes cannot replace military or police forces but only act in their support. Not only do gendarmes not remove the need for military involvement in extreme disorder but their introduction represents a militarization of policing that may create more problems than it solves, sending the wrong signals in processes of reconciliation and democratization. Their use also increases the likelihood of coordination problems between the various forces.[35]

Political concerns and the interference of national governments that plagues multinational peace operations can also be expected to create disruptions in mixed military–police chains of command.

---

[34] Personal communications with UNMIK Police staff, Stockholm, May 2001, and Berlin, June 2001.
[35] Hills (note 3), pp. 92ff.

Even without micromanaging national governments, primacy can become a problematic issue if a web of 'functional relationships' does emerge and weaken the military–police dichotomy. Whether it is the military or the civilian police that take the lead in a given situation will have to be tried and tested in practice. At the level of mission heads, a case can be made for the military commander and the police commissioner enjoying equal standing in any executive policing operation. In the same way as a multinational force consists of national units below a certain level of organization, a 'mixed' chain of command may not be the most effective choice at the tactical level. Although not directly an example of military–police cooperation, the investigation of crimes against humanity in East Timor is an example of a task that required consistent questioning and handling of evidence and testimonies, rather than shifting authority and primacy between the military and the civilian police.[36] A related area in which chain-of-command and primacy issues are especially problematic is intelligence gathering and sharing. The experiences of joint actions, such as high-profile arrests, in Kosovo and East Timor will provide more insight into appropriate levels of integration, especially at different levels of violence.

The credibility of each component depends not only on its own performance, but just as much on how well they work together. When enforcing the law in war-torn societies, military and police forces face powerful and highly organized culprits or 'spoilers'.[37] Without a well-functioning command structure that is flexible enough to allow the component forces their autonomy and ability to respond, while at the same time enabling smooth joint operations—which by necessity are more likely to take place in a hostile environment and therefore require a united front—the international effort will be outmanoeuvred by its local adversaries. There is a fine balance between deriving benefits from flexibility and a differentiated division of labour, on the one hand, and undermining the hard-won cooperation and cohesion between the military and the civilian police, on the other.

[36] Human Rights Watch (note 20), pp. 2ff.
[37] On spoilers, see also chapter 3 in this volume.

IV. Conclusions

Effective military–police cooperation has to contend with major unresolved challenges, including those of command structures and joint planning. While there appears to be an awareness of a joint responsibility for public security and a willingness to find solutions to these challenges, the solutions themselves may be at a level that defies generalization and institutionalization.

This chapter has called for a detailed understanding of policing functions and of how the military can support their execution, as well as for a recognition of national differences and complex institutional constellations. Together these considerations point to a highly complex puzzle of scenarios, organizational structures and political concerns. There is, however, no reason not to try to improve cooperation by putting some pieces of the puzzle into place and thereby facing recalcitrant political leaders and other spoilers—who tend to be most active in undermining law and order in a conflict area—in a more coherent and determined effort.

Having argued for a complex approach, it is also worth restating the simple basic truth of military–police cooperation. 'Providing a secure environment' is obviously a task that is akin to traditional peacekeeping and accepted military roles, but other tasks—first and foremost the investigation of crimes and the training of indigenous police forces—will have to remain in the hands of the international police.

When it comes down to it, there is no danger of the military drowning in a police role, as there are a host of jobs it simply cannot do. While it is clearly desirable that the military develop a greater understanding of the needs and modes of operation of the civilian police component—and vice versa—the military will not have to retrain or prepare to replace the civilian police in peace operations. It is also in the interest of the civilian police contingent that the credibility of the military as an effective muscular back-up and as a stabilizing force in-theatre is not diluted. The key to improving military–police cooperation is developing effective relationships in which both sides support and complement each other without neglecting or undermining their own roles within the peace operation—that is, for the military, providing a secure environment and, for the civilian police, promoting the rule of law.

6. National police training within an executive police operation

Robert M. Perito

I. Introduction

The fact that international civilian police have executive authority does not obviate the traditional requirement for training and mentoring local police. 'Training and restructuring form the essential foundation for any executive policing operation, in that these activities are the ones that ultimately build local law enforcement capacity and eventually allow the international mission to go home.'[1] In fact, all executive missions eventually transform into monitoring and training missions. Executive policing is undertaken concurrently with efforts to establish an indigenous police force.[2] This view is reflected in the *Civilian Police Principles and Guidelines* issued by the UN Department of Peace-keeping Operations (DPKO).[3] In its guidance to UN police commissioners for conducting UN Civilian Police (CivPol) operations, the DPKO advises that, in operations where UN CivPols have executive authority, training and mentoring/monitoring programmes are among the principal methods for managing the transition of authority to local police.[4]

While UN CivPols were first used in the Congo crisis of 1960–64,[5] the two examples of UN executive police missions—in Kosovo and East Timor—both date from 1999. Here, the UN established transitional authorities that were responsible for civil administration, including law enforcement and the training of indigenous police. Responsibility for training was handled differently in Kosovo and East Timor, with different results. In Kosovo, the UN delegated police training to the Organization for Security and Co-operation in Europe

---

[1] Hansen, A., International Institute for Strategic Studies, *From Congo to Kosovo: Civilian Police in Peace Operations*, Adelphi Paper no. 343 (Oxford University Press: Oxford, 2002).
[2] Hansen (note 1).
[3] United Nations, Department of Peace-keeping Operations, *United Nations Civilian Police Principles and Guidelines* (UN: New York, 2001).
[4] *United Nations Civilian Police Principles and Guidelines* (note 3).
[5] United Nations, *The Blue Helmets: A Review of United Nations Peace-keeping*, 3rd edn (United Nations: New York, 1996), pp. 641–48.

(OSCE), a regional organization. In East Timor the UN provided the police training programme. As of December 2001, 4392 new police officers had graduated from the OSCE-sponsored Kosovo Police Service School. In East Timor 1450 cadets—about half of its projected target of 3000 police officers by April 2003—had graduated from the UN-administered Timor Lorosa'e Police Training College.[6]

II. The Kosovo Police Service School

The UN Interim Administration Mission in Kosovo (UNMIK) was set up on 10 June 1999 by UN Security Council Resolution 1244. Authority for training a local police force was provided in a single sentence, which also provided executive authority for a 4700-member UN Civilian Police Force (the UNMIK Police). The sentence stated that the responsibilities of UNMIK would include 'maintaining civil law and order, including establishing local police forces [sic] and meanwhile through the deployment of international police personnel to serve in Kosovo'.[7] The draft agreement proposed in February 1999 by the Contact Group at the Rambouillet peace talks had provided for an ethnic-Albanian 'Communal Police Force' with locally-based units commanded by officers chosen by local councils.[8] Instead, UNMIK opted for an indigenous police force under centralized UN administration, the Kosovo Police Service (KPS). Under the international division of responsibility in Kosovo, the UN is responsible for civil administration and the OSCE for institutional development. The UNMIK Police supervise KPS operations, while the OSCE Mission Department of Police Education and Development is responsible for training and professional development.[9]

The OSCE's responsibility for training the KPS grew out of its activities in Kosovo before the 1999 NATO bombing campaign

---

[6] Statistics provided by the UN Department of Peace-keeping Operations, Civilian Police Division, 1 Dec. 2001.

[7] UN Security Council Resolution 1244, 10 June 1999, para. 11(i). Resolution 1244 is reproduced in appendix A in this volume.

[8] Draft Interim Agreement for Peace and Self-Government in Kosovo, annex II (Police and Security), available at URL <http://www.balkanaction.org/paper/dkia.html>. The draft agreement between representatives of the Federal Republic of Yugoslavia (FRY), the Government of the Republic of Serbia and the Kosovo ethnic-Albanians was never signed.

[9] Papworth, T. and Wiharta, S., 'Policing Europe: European policing? The challenge of coordination in international policing', Report of the workshop hosted by the Stockholm International Peace Research Institute (SIPRI), Stockholm, 4–5 May 2001, p. 8.

against the Federal Republic of Yugoslavia (FRY). Under an October 1998 agreement between US envoy Richard Holbrooke and then FRY President Slobodan Milosevic, the OSCE provided the Kosovo Verification Mission (KVM), an international force of 2000 unarmed observers, including 500 police.[10] Before the KVM was evacuated from Kosovo and while the bombing campaign was in progress, the OSCE developed a police training programme. It also developed plans for recruiting, vetting and selecting potential trainees. Much of the work was done by the US Department of Justice International Criminal Investigative Training Assistance Program (ICITAP). When hostilities ended, the results of this extensive pre-planning effort were made available to UNMIK and used by the UN and the OSCE in programme implementation. This advanced work made it possible for the Kosovo Police Service School (KPSS) to begin training within two months after NATO forces—the Kosovo Force (KFOR)—arrived in Kosovo.[11]

The KPSS inducted its first group of 176 trainees on 6 September 1999. The goal was to train a force of 4000 police officers with proportional representation from the main ethnic groups, minorities and women. The OSCE provided US$6.5 million for the complete renovation of the school, which was little more than a shell when it was first occupied. The KPSS was transformed into a state-of-the-art training facility with an annual budget of $15.5 million in 2000 and $13.5 million in 2001. (These figures do not include the salaries of KPSS international staff, which were paid directly by donor governments.) Located in Vucitrin, the campus has capacity to house 678 students, 28 classrooms, two gymnasiums, a weights room, a modern mess hall which can feed 950 students and 450 staff, laundry facilities, a warehouse, an armoury, a medical clinic, administrative offices and a physical plant capable of operating independently of local power and water resources.[12]

When it became fully operational in March 2000, the KPSS had a staff of 208 international police instructors from 24 OSCE member

[10] Meyers, S., '2,000 monitors go to Kosovo, but their power is unclear', *New York Times*, 15 Oct. 1998, p. A6.

[11] Bennett, S., 'Police training in Kosovo', Testimony presented at the Helsinki Commission Hearing on Civilian Police and Police Training in Post-Conflict OSCE Areas, Washington, DC, 5 Sep. 2001, available at URL <www.csce.gov/witness.cfm?briefing Td=197&testimony>.

[12] OSCE Mission in Kosovo, 'Kosovo Police Service School fact sheet', Pristina, Jan. 2001.

states, 265 local staff and a complement of over 600 cadets in training at any one time. UNMIK Police served as field training officers (FTOs) for the new police officers after graduation. Initially all UNMIK Police officers received two days of instruction at the school in FTO duties. When it became clear that not all CivPols were adept at this function, a contingent of UNMIK Police 'mentors' was identified and they received FTO training.[13] During training, cadets live and study together in a completely integrated environment. The school seeks to emphasize the potential for multi-ethnic professional cooperation, including both sexes. Today, the KPSS and the KPS are the only multi-ethnic institutions functioning in Kosovo, although Serb police serve only in their own ethnic communities.

Training is built around three broad themes of professional development.

The first is basic police skills. Cadets undergo an initial eight weeks of instruction at the school. The curriculum includes the fundamentals of police patrol, criminal investigation, interview techniques, report writing, traffic control, gathering forensic evidence, relevant law, defensive tactics, the use of firearms, first aid and the skills related to the special needs of police in Kosovo. Topics in this latter area include conflict intervention, the handling of refugees, mine awareness and policing in a democratic society. Courses are taught in a manner that highlights respect for international standards of human rights. International police instructors lecture in English with interpretation in Albanian and Serbian by local language assistants.[14]

After graduating from the basic police course, officers undergo an additional 19 weeks of structured field training provided by UNMIK Police FTOs. This on-the-job training emphasizes the practical application of skills learned in the classroom. During this period, KPS officers also receive an additional 80 hours of classroom training aimed at improving competence and the ability to perform the full range of police services. KPSS staff present these in-service courses at one of three regional training centres or at the school for officers serving in Pristina and Mitrovica. After a total of 27 weeks of classroom and field training, KPS officers are eligible for UNMIK certification and assignment.[15]

[13] OSCE Mission in Kosovo, *Kosovo Police Service School Annual Report 2000* (Pristina, 2001), pp. 1–2.

[14] Bennett (note 11).

[15] 'Kosovo Police Service School fact sheet' (note 12).

The second theme is training in supervision, management and specialized skills. Short courses have been developed to train 'first-line' supervisors and middle-level managers. Upon completing these courses, officers are added to a pool of possible future leaders of the KPS. At the same time, specialized courses have been developed in driving a police vehicle, criminal investigation, traffic management, accident investigation and drug identification. There is also a re-qualification programme in firearms, defensive tactics and first aid. Officers rotate back to the KPSS or to one of the regional training centres to take these courses.

The third theme is creating the capacity within the KPS to sustain a professional level of training on its own. An initial group of KPS officers have been certified as instructors and now teach at the school. A cadre of KPS field trainers has also begun taking over this function from the UNMIK Police.

On 15 September 2001, the KPSS met its initial goal of training 4106 new members of the KPS. Graduates included 356 ethnic Serbs, 313 from other minorities and 773 women. In the same period, the KPSS trained 2103 UNMIK police officers as FTOs.[16] Current projections are for 1500 additional officers to complete basic training by December 2002.[17]

III. The Timor Lorosa'e Police Training College

In contrast to the case of Kosovo, where the OSCE did extensive pre-mission planning, in East Timor the UN had little opportunity to prepare for police training. In the wake of the violence that followed the 30 August 1999 independence referendum, the UN Security Council, acting under Chapter VII of the UN Charter, adopted Resolution 1272 establishing the UN Transitional Administration in East Timor (UNTAET) on 25 October 1999.[18] UNTAET was responsible for all aspects of civil administration, including the administration of justice. Among its principal components was a UN CivPol force 1640 strong. On 31 January 2001, Security Council Resolution 1338 reaffirmed the

---

[16] Statistics provided by the Kosovo Police Service School, 14 Oct. 2001.

[17] Bennett (note 11).

[18] UN Security Council Resolution 1272, 25 Oct. 1999, reproduced in appendix A in this volume.

CivPol mandate and emphasized the need to expedite the training of an indigenous police force.

A 'panorama of devastation' greeted the UN in Dili, the capital of East Timor. Most buildings, including schools, hospitals and government offices, had been destroyed. Transport, communications and the judicial infrastructure were in ruins. UN efforts to train a new police force began from scratch.[19] UNTAET finalized work on the selection criteria for the new East Timor Police Service (ETPS) in January 2000 and application forms were made available to applicants. Recruitment was done through local 'law and order committees' which were organized by CivPols with the assistance of 800 former members of the Indonesian National Police who served in a Police Assistance Group (PAG). A total of 13,000 applications were received. About 400 members of the PAG were also able to qualify for admission to the police-training programme.[20]

Training at the East Timor Police Training College (ETPTC) began on 27 March 2000 with the first class of 50 recruits. Its mission was to provide basic and specialized training in police skills to both recruits and sworn police officers. Local police training had been part of earlier CivPol mandates, but this was the UN's most ambitious effort without substantial help from bilateral donors. Once training was under way, the UN transformed the campus from a group of dilapidated buildings into a modern institution with adequate teaching and residential facilities. The college is staffed by 46 CivPol officers and provides basic training for five classes of 50 cadets each. The number of cadets is limited by a shortage of funding, classrooms and staff. A $15 million shortfall in donor contributions to the UN Trust Fund for East Timor left only $4.3 million for the police-training programme. Of this $2.6 million was used to renovate the facility.[21]

The ETPTC director reports to the CivPol Commissioner. CivPol instructors are assigned to the college by the UNTAET Personnel Section and represent a cross-section of the countries participating in the UNTAET mission. Not all the CivPols assigned to the college are trained instructors or have prior teaching experience. Lectures are

[19] Strohmeyer, H., 'Policing the peace: post-conflict judicial system reconstruction in the case of East Timor', Paper presented at the International Peace Academy and Jane's Information Group Seminar on Peacekeeping and Peace Support Operations, New York, 2–3 Nov. 2000, pp. 1–2.

[20] Author's interview with A. Lopes, UN Department of Peace-keeping Operations, Civilian Police Division, UN Headquarters, New York, 1 Dec. 2001.

[21] Lopes (note 20).

given in English with translation into Bahasa Indonesia by local language assistants.[22]

ETPS recruits undergo a 12-week basic training programme at the college followed by three months of field training under the supervision of CivPol FTOs. Courses are presented in human rights, ethics, community policing, crime prevention, criminal investigation, sex crimes, domestic violence, patrolling, mediation, defensive tactics, drill, physical fitness, driving, law, first aid, arrest procedures, report writing, traffic control and firearms. FTOs are also trained at the college in mentoring and monitoring new police officers. Field training focuses on the practical application of information learned in the classroom. A four-week Intensive Transitional Training (ITT) or fast-track programme has been developed for cadets with prior law enforcement experience as members of the Indonesian National Police Force. The course has the same standards as the basic training course with a significant component in community policing and human rights. Officers taking the ITT course also participate in the FTO programme.[23]

The USA, through ICITAP, established a training assistance programme in late 2000 to provide ETPTC graduates with courses in instructor development, curriculum development and training management. A number of ETPS officers have completed the instructor development course and have been assigned to the staff of the Police College. ICITAP has also trained ETPS supervisors and managers through courses in police supervision and management principles, professional standards, the management of civil disorder and forensic investigation. UNTAET uses these courses as a requirement for the promotion of ETPS officers. The USA has donated police equipment, including forensic investigation kits and riot control equipment.[24] Bilateral assistance has also been provided by Australia, Japan and Portugal. The ETPTC does not have an in-service training programme, nor does it have a re-qualification programme to help officers maintain required skill levels in the use of firearms, defensive tactics and first aid.

---

[22] UNTAET Civilian Police, 'East Timor Police Service', Dili, Sep. 2001, pp. 7–8.

[23] UNTAET Civilian Police, 'A glimpse on the Timor Lorosa'e Police Training College', Delta Comoro, 2000, pp. 2–3.

[24] 'East Timor Police Service' (note 22), p. 9.

IV. Training issues

Length of training

The training and development of indigenous civilian police forces is a multi-year effort that requires international police officers who are more than just law enforcement professionals. They must also be experts in building institutions, establishing police academies, instruction and curriculum development, creating police departments and designing systems of law enforcement service delivery based on democratic principles of community-oriented policing. In this aspect of their work, UN Civilian Police forces have been handicapped by the UN's failure until recently to specifically recruit police instructors, police academy directors, police administrators and strategic planners.

Short-term assignments and rapid turnover of personnel also handicap UN CivPol involvement in training and institutional development. This is especially true in executive police missions, where CivPol leadership and resources are necessarily focused on operational law enforcement, particularly at the beginning of a mission. In addition, training and institution building require a high level of political will on the part of the international community, including the fortitude to withstand pressure from local factions who seek to influence the composition and organization of the new police force.[25]

In executive police missions there are political and practical imperatives to establish an indigenous police force quickly and to speed up the training and development process in order to get as many indigenous police officers on the street as rapidly as possible. Politically, it is important for the UN interim authority to demonstrate that it is not an occupation force and that its goal is to empower local citizens. Practically, indigenous police provide a 'force multiplier' by increasing the number of police officers available to patrol and provide area security. CivPol missions are inherently slow to deploy. In missions where CivPols provide the only police presence the use of local manpower to maintain public order can be critical. The assistance of local police officers is helpful as CivPols normally do not speak the local languages and are unfamiliar with local culture and geography. The

[25] Call, C. and Barnett, M., 'Looking for a few good cops: peacekeeping, peacebuilding and UN civilian police', Paper presented at the International Studies Association's 38th Annual Meeting, Toronto, Canada, 18–22 Mar. 1997, pp. 1–3, 22–27.

creation of an indigenous police force that is capable of providing sustainable security is also a critical component of the 'exit strategy' of the international police mission.

A basic training programme designed to give raw recruits a minimum understanding of policing skills and the law normally takes between six and 12 months.[26] In Kosovo, UNMIK limited the period of classroom instruction for the first KPS class to five weeks because the snail-like pace of CivPol deployment had resulted in a critical shortage of police personnel. After the first graduation ceremony, however, the new KPS officers had to return to class for an additional three weeks of remedial instruction and to make up time lost due to water shortages and power failures.[27] The KPSS basic training programme for all subsequent classes was extended to eight weeks. In East Timor, the basic training programme was limited to three months. This raised questions among CivPol instructors and ETPS cadets about the problems such abbreviated training would cause when newly graduated police officers were deployed.

In both Kosovo and East Timor, police training is done using consecutive translation, which reduces by nearly one-half the actual time available for instruction. When the difficulty of understanding new terminology and concepts is included, effective communication between instructors and students can be a challenge, particularly when training is accelerated to meet political or security-related deadlines.[28]

Recruitment and vetting

Among the primary determinants of the length of police training are the education, experience, age and motivation of the students. In a perfect world, application to the police academy would be open to all and only the best-qualified would be appointed. In the aftermath of ethnic conflict and in the confusion of reconstruction, hard realities and political expediency are at least as important as merit in determining who receives police training.

[26] Hartz, H., 'CIVPOL: the UN instrument for police reform', *International Peacekeeping*, vol. 6, no. 4 (winter 1999), p. 33.

[27] OSCE Mission in Kosovo, 'First class graduates from Kosovo Police Service School', Press Release, 16 Oct. 1999, URL <http://www.usia.gov/cgi-bin/washfi...=/products/washfile/newsitem.shtml>.

[28] Mobekk, E., 'Policing peace operations: United Nations civilian police in East Timor', Monograph for the John D. and Catherine T. MacArthur Foundation Program on Peace and International Co-operation, King's College, London, Oct. 2001, p. 48.

A critical aspect of the recruiting process is the vetting of those selected to determine whether they are guilty of previous criminal behaviour or abuse of human rights. This is particularly important for senior officers who can influence the attitudes and behaviour of more junior officers and the police rank and file. Even in executive police operations where there is no existing indigenous police force, police organizations reflect the customs and traditions of the past. This is true if only because individuals with prior police experience are always in short supply. Suitable former fighters cannot be wasted or safely excluded. 'The police evolve from previous structures shaped by historical inheritance, political pressures, specific events and professional concerns.'[29] Investigating the background of police recruits can be challenging enough in Western countries where there is ready access to government registries, law enforcement records, school files, credit references, newspaper files and other sources. Such efforts are nearly impossible following violent civil conflicts in which records have been destroyed or not kept for extended periods, or in rural areas with limited government infrastructure.

In Kosovo and East Timor, efforts were made to establish reasonable selection criteria and to engage in a vigorous recruitment and vetting process. In Kosovo, members of the first class were selected from a pool of 28,995 applications.[30] Candidates were required to be at least 21 years of age, have at least a secondary education, be physically and mentally fit, have no criminal history and be residents of Kosovo. The applicant screening process, which was conducted by a joint team of law enforcement professionals from UNMIK and the OSCE, involved an oral interview, a written examination, a psychological test, a medical examination and a physical agility test. It also included a background investigation conducted by UN and OSCE teams which visited home towns to interview people who knew prospective students. Given the prolonged period of educational discrimination against ethnic Albanians by the FRY authorities, it is not surprising that the applicants' level of education was a significant problem. Nearly 80 per cent of the applicants failed to qualify because they were unable to pass the written examination.[31]

---

[29] Hill, A., *Policing Africa: Internal Security and the Limits of Liberalization* (Lynne Rienner: Boulder, Colo., 2000), p. 11.
[30] *Kosovo Police Service School Annual Report 2000* (note 13).
[31] Papworth and Wiharta (note 9).

Once the screening process was completed, political objectives and understandings between the UN and Kosovar special-interest groups played a major role in determining who was appointed to the KPSS. UNMIK had agreed with local political leaders that 50 per cent of KPS recruits would be KLA veterans. It had also agreed with the association of former Kosovar Yugoslav National Police officers (who had served during the period of local autonomy before 1989) that its members would make up 25 per cent of the KPS. The UN set goals of 15 per cent for Serb and other minority participation and 20 per cent for women. The majority of those selected were outstanding individuals, but collectively these quotas excluded nearly all non-affiliated, ethnic-Albanian males who generally had the highest educational levels and often were otherwise most qualified.[32]

In East Timor, applicants to the ETPS completed a four-stage process that included a written application, an interview, review of the application in Dili and local publication of applicants' names so that citizens could voice objections on grounds of prior militia or criminal activity. Prior to the interview, however, CivPols relied heavily on recommendations from the National Council of Timorese Resistance and local law and order committees. Inevitably local leaders sought to influence the process and to promote particular individuals. Special exceptions were also made for former members of the Indonesian National Police who joined the PAG. They helped both CivPols and the village law and order committees with the selection process and probably also influenced decisions on selection.[33]

Doctrine and curriculum

The UN and bilateral donors agree that new indigenous police services should operate on the basis of democratic principles, employ community policing techniques and aim at the ideal of professionalism. Democratic policing has two essential features—responsiveness and accountability. Community policing involves establishing close ties with the community, public service and responsiveness to community concerns. Professionalism defines norms in value-neutral terms of effectiveness, making them less sensitive politically.[34] Beyond these

[32] Author's interview with S. Bennett at the Kosovo Police Service School, Dec. 2000.
[33] Mobekk (note 28), p. 46.
[34] Hansen (note 1). For a discussion of democratic and community policing see chapter 4 in this volume.

general principles, however, there is no agreement on common doctrine, nor is there a UN curriculum for training local police. In addition, CivPol monitoring or executive police missions are not recruited for or designed to provide police training. UN policy makers simply seem to assume that CivPol missions will be able to train the local police in addition to performing their other duties.[35]

In the absence of a UN doctrine, curriculum and professional training cadre, CivPol officers have taught classes on the basis of their own, highly varied experience, materials brought from their own countries and recycled lesson plans from earlier UN missions. In some cases bilateral donors and regional organizations with experience in post-conflict police training and a cadre of professional trainers have provided comprehensive programmes tailored to local conditions.[36] This was true in Kosovo, where ICITAP provided the basic training curriculum. In East Timor, the ETPTC began using curricula recycled from earlier UN missions and training materials developed locally by individual CivPol officers. This placed the East Timor programme at a disadvantage, especially in its first year of operation. It also led to inconsistencies in the classroom and in the Field Training Programme, where training was left to the initiative of individual CivPol officers who had little experience as trainers and were fully occupied with operational law enforcement.[37]

In addition to providing basic services, indigenous police may be required to provide riot control, serve as border guards, provide courtroom security or temporarily serve as prison personnel. These responsibilities require specialized training. It is important that this training is conducted by the police academy and in a manner consistent with other aspects of the police-training programme. In Kosovo, KPS officers who were selected by UNMIK to serve as border guards were initially trained by German CivPol border guards with no coordination with the KPSS. Eventually this situation was corrected and the KPSS added border control training to its Advanced and Specialized Training Division. In East Timor, a paramilitary 'rapid reaction unit' of ETPS officers was trained and equipped by ICITAP.

[35] Hartz (note 26), p. 33.
[36] Holm, T., 'CIVPOL operations in Eastern Slavonia', *International Peacekeeping*, vol. 6, no. 4 (winter 1999), p. 147.
[37] Mobekk (note 28), p. 49.

V. Institutional development

While the task of training indigenous police is daunting, creating the organizational infrastructure for a new police force is an even greater challenge. Institutional development involves creating administrative structures, standards, procedures and codes of conduct; deciding personnel regulations, including salary schedules; and determining force levels, mission and long-term objectives. The goal is the creation of a professional, humane civilian police force that operates with respect for internationally recognized human rights and the rule of law. Such a force must be composed of individuals from diverse ethnic, religious and political groups who will protect citizens and enforce the law with impartiality.[38]

In most cases, provisions for creating an indigenous police service are not detailed in the peace agreement and it is left to the international civilian police force to improvise solutions under less than ideal circumstances. This is particularly true as peace settlements normally do not identify the financial resources for implementing police reform and restructuring, which is more than simply transferring police skills from the international civilian police to a 'rookie' indigenous force.

The most serious challenges to fledgling police services derive from weak judicial institutions and from traditions of intimidation and authoritarianism in society. Police reform must be a component of a comprehensive effort to reform the entire judicial system, which includes prosecutors, courts and prisons. A competent judicial system is necessary to prevent impunity from prosecution and to ensure that justice is an effective alternative to the renewal of armed conflict.[39]

End-state and infrastructure

In training an indigenous police force from scratch, logic would dictate that the first decision would involve the end-state: What type of force are we trying to create? Will it be a national police force with a centralized command structure, a decentralized communal police with autonomous units reporting to local leaders, or something in between?

---

[38] Call, C. and Stanley, W., 'Protecting the people: public security choices after civil wars', *Global Governance*, no. 7 (2001), pp. 151–72.

[39] Neild, R., 'Democratic police reforms in war-torn societies', *Conflict, Security and Development*, vol. 1, no. 1 (winter 2001), pp. 21–23.

The answer may be found in the peace agreement or relevant Security Council resolutions, but not always. In Kosovo, failure to determine a political end-state has negatively affected the training and institutional development of the KPS. After field training, members of the KPS are assigned to UNMIK police stations as 'auxiliaries' of the UNMIK Police. As it is uncertain whether the KPS will become a national or a provincial police force, the UN has not begun building its organization and rank structure. UNMIK has given little attention to developing the capacity within the KPS for finance, administration, management, logistics, human resources and information technology, and it has not been decided how many officers are needed for each police function. Consequently, the KPSS has been limited to providing generic management training to 'pools' of police officers who could serve as first-line supervisors, middle-level managers and executives when the UN makes such appointments.[40]

This is not true in East Timor, where it has been clear from the outset that the ETPS will be a national police service with a centralized command structure. The ETPS commissioner, five subcommissioners and 28 superintendents have been trained and are in place. In addition, the UN is committed to reducing the number of CivPols as the ETPS is deployed and demonstrates its competence.[41]

Law

While a police cadet's training involves learning a set of basic technical skills, his or her education is heavily influenced by the applicable criminal law and code of criminal procedures. For example, the manner in which a suspect is taken into custody is determined by the laws and regulations governing what constitutes a legal arrest. A substantial part of an effective police training programme should, therefore, be devoted to instruction in law and procedures, so the police officer understands the legal basis and limits of his authority. Where there is a UN transitional administration, the question of what the local law is can be difficult to resolve.[42]

---

[40] Eide, D. and Holm, T., 'Postscript: towards executive authority policing? The lessons of Kosovo', *International Peacekeeping*, vol. 6, no. 4 (winter 1999), p. 217.

[41] 'East Timor Police Service' (note 22), p. 6.

[42] For a discussion of how this problem was addressed in Kosovo and East Timor see chapter 2 in this volume.

Relation to the justice system

It is generally recognized that police cannot operate effectively without the support of the two other parts of the 'judicial triad'—the courts and the prisons. In executive police missions it is particularly important for indigenous police training to include instruction on how police function within the judicial system in a democratic society. Their position within this system can vary widely depending on whether the legal system is based on English common law, French civil law or another legal system such as sharia. Police training must impart an understanding of the officer's responsibilities to the rest of the judicial system so that investigations and interrogations will produce evidence that is accepted by the courts and useful in obtaining convictions. In Kosovo, the prolonged dispute over applicable law and the failure of the judicial and penal system to function beyond a very rudimentary level initially meant that over 40 per cent of those detained were released and few were brought to trial despite ample indications of guilt.[43] In East Timor, legal confusion prompted the continued use of traditional communal mechanisms, which sometimes contravened international human rights law.[44] Even if police are better trained and more effective, law and order will not improve if the other parts of the judicial system remain in crisis.

VI. Summary and conclusions

The training of indigenous police in peace operations is resource-intensive. In a post-conflict environment, it requires the commitment of large amounts of money, manpower and material to rebuild academy infrastructure, provide equipment and administrative staff, develop curricula and provide instructors. In executive police missions, competition for resources is particularly acute. This was evident in East Timor, where shortfalls in contributions to the UN Trust Fund severely limited the resources available for police training. In Kosovo, the problem was resolved by delegating responsibility for training and development to the OSCE, a regional organization with superior resources. While this option may not always be available, it should be

---

[43] Eide and Holm (note 40), p. 218.
[44] Mobekk (note 28), p. 62.

considered. If necessary, the UN could delegate responsibility to a 'coalition of the willing' that would have the required resources.

Police training and institutional development are a long-term undertaking. It takes at least five years to create a police force from scratch. Here again the UN is at a disadvantage compared to regional organizations and bilateral donors. In an executive police mission, emphasis is necessarily placed on meeting operational, short-term needs. With their short assignments, frequent turnover and focus on an 'exit strategy', CivPols are ill suited for training a new police force. This is another reason to consider assigning this function to a regional organization, a group of states or a single country with the interest and resources to stay the course.

Police training requires agreement on common doctrine and methodology and a cadre of professional instructors. Beyond a general agreement on basic principles and subjects that should be taught, there is no common understanding within the UN on doctrine, methodology or course content for police training programmes. Police organizations and practice vary widely even among Western democracies. The common practice of training a few officers in various national police academies only creates confusion when they return to duty. Training should be done in-country at one facility so that all trainees have a common experience. Optimally, one international organization should have responsibility for all aspects of training—classroom instruction, field training and in-service courses. This would allow the entire training sequence to be systematic and standardized.

CivPol executive policing missions are not equipped with professional training units or designed to develop new police institutions. Local police training is a highly specialized function that cannot be done as a simple 'add-on' to operational duties. The UN practice of universal recruitment works against consensus on the content of training programmes for indigenous police. Unless the UN Civilian Police Division develops a specialized unit for indigenous police training, this task is best left to bilateral donors, regional organizations or coalitions of like-minded states. This also applies to the use of CivPols as field training officers. A core group of FTO officers with the interest and appropriate backgrounds should be identified and receive specialized training before performing this function.

In executive police missions where there is no pre-existing local police force, it is particularly important that indigenous police training is part of a comprehensive programme to develop the entire judicial system. While skill training is important, police training should provide the cadet with an understanding of criminal law and the procedures, standards and codes of conduct of his department. Laws, procedures and standards must be available before training begins even if they are prepared in advance by the UN and used only until local equivalents can be developed. It is equally important that local police training includes instruction on how police in a democracy relate to other parts of the justice system and to civil society. This should be part of the curriculum, but cadets should also be exposed to prosecutors, judges, penal officers and representatives of civil society during their training. This is particularly true in situations where police may have to provide courtroom security, serve as prison guards or otherwise protect or support other parts of the judicial system.

7. Transitions to local authority

*Eric Scheye**

I. Introduction

Not since the end of World War II has the international community been confronted with the rule-of-law challenges it has faced since 1999 in Kosovo and East Timor—to build and install a new law enforcement regime after a period when the international community exercised full executive authority and functioned as the legitimate government and transitional administration. The international community has been asked to help in the rebuilding of domestic police agencies after a period of internal conflict—in Bosnia and Herzegovina, Cambodia, Eastern Slavonia, El Salvador and Haiti—but the task of transferring full executive authority to a brand-new law enforcement regime under domestic civilian control is qualitatively different. The fact that this transfer will occur under the authority and direction of the United Nations Department of Peace-keeping Operations (DPKO) rather than under the auspices of an occupying foreign power or powers marks these transfers as fundamentally different from those that occurred after World War II.

Overlooking the obvious economic, cultural and ethnic differences between Kosovo and East Timor (and one glaring political difference—Kosovo's unsettled political end-state), the DPKO's tasks in the UN Interim Administration Mission in Kosovo (UNMIK) and the UN Transitional Administration in East Timor (UNTAET) are technically identical. In both, in addition to exercising executive authority for an interim period, the DPKO is responsible for establishing a well trained and fully equipped professional local police agency, able to perform its duties independently and in accordance with international standards of human rights and the principles of democratic policing. Furthermore, the new law enforcement agencies are to be fully self-sustainable as soon as the international civilian police are withdrawn.[1]

[1] Author's interviews with UNMIK and UNTAET staff, Feb., July, Aug. and Dec. 2001.

* This chapter is partly based on interviews with UNMIK and UNTAET personnel carried out in Feb., July, Aug. and Dec. 2001. The views expressed are those of the author and do not necessarily reflect those of the United Nations.

For analytical clarity, the objectives of the police operations can be broken down into three elements: (*a*) developing professional police officers (the individual); (*b*) establishing an accountable, transparent and rights-respecting law enforcement institution (the institution); and (*c*) integrating that institution within the larger rule-of-law system under responsible democratic civilian control, both formal and informal (the relationship between institutions, including civil society).

From this perspective it is clear that the building of local East Timorese and Kosovo law enforcement agencies and the transfer of executive law enforcement functions from the UN to them is not purely a police exercise. Fundamental legal, financial and public administration questions are also at stake. A delicate balance between these elements must therefore be achieved before, during and after the transition of executive authority, for discrepancies either between the three levels or between the various disciplines could easily result in a deteriorating law-and-order environment, which would impede the peaceful development of the territory in question. For example, the credibility of a police agency will be undermined if the alleged perpetrators of illegal activity are not justly and fairly prosecuted. Similarly, the legitimacy of a law enforcement service will be eroded if its operations are seen to be either too subservient or unresponsive to the dictates of civilian political masters or the communities to whom it provides a service. Finally, the effectiveness of a police service will be destroyed if it is not adequately supported financially by the public administration of which it is but one institution.

At the same time, it must be noted that the establishment of an indigenous police service and the transfer of power to it are an inherently political enterprise and take place in an environment in which the realm of politics is itself contested, for no recognized and capable local government exists. To build a police service when the fundamental rules of the political game remain basically 'up for grabs' or, at the very least, there are no other legitimate functioning political institutions is an exercise in futility. The re-establishment of politics cannot be achieved on the back of local law enforcement. Rather police services are but one integral element of governance and can only be successfully recreated in parallel with the reintroduction of other key government systems. Local political institutions cannot be developed in linear fashion but must be grafted in sequence onto a society's political body.

II. Constraints

Before describing the parameters within which a transfer of executive authority can take place and the methods by which UNTAET and UNMIK envisage it will occur, it is appropriate to review a number of constraints under which the transfer will take place. They can come in various guises and configurations, but most, if not all, peace operations will face similar circumstances.

Historical

The international community will only assume executive authority and that authority will only need to be transferred back later to local structures after the territory in question has undergone a long period of conflict and its governmental structure has collapsed. The costs of the conflict will have been enormous, and not only in terms of lives lost and widespread physical devastation. The human capital of the territory may have been depleted by death, displacement, emigration and a prolonged absence of educational opportunities. An entire cohort may have reached maturity knowing little else but the imperatives of conflict and oppression, and having few skills by which to pursue gainful peacetime employment. The effects this can have on the ability to build a domestic law enforcement agency from scratch are profound. There is also likely to be a serious lack of supervisory, administrative and managerial talent and experience.

The demographic characteristics of the area may also have changed significantly. Conflict often accelerates urbanization and, concomitantly, rural depopulation. Such population movements not only disrupt the previously acknowledged patterns of law enforcement but also shift the domestic political balance of power by increasing the leverage of those leaders who control the fortunes of the displaced populations. The issue here is not which domestic leadership wields power. Rather, those wielding local power may well have gained ascendancy because of the war; their continued enjoyment of the prerogatives of power may be dependent on the unsavoury and often illegal methods by which they acquired it, and the legitimacy of their exercise of political authority may be at best tentative. The political decisions made during the transition period may often be made according to the personal short-term political calculations of a political class that lacks a secure base, and may therefore not be sustainable over time.

It is also likely that previous methods of law enforcement, before the conflict as well as during it, were profoundly discriminatory, brutal and corrupt. Policing powers may have been exercised more for the private benefit of a narrow segment of the population—ethnically, religiously or politically defined—than for the general public welfare. The historical legacy of policing in the minds and practices of the public that is to be served, not to mention the local officers who will eventually be entrusted with police powers, may thus work against the establishment of an accountable, transparent and rights-respecting law enforcement agency. The local population may, for instance, want the police to act physically and brutally against alleged perpetrators of crimes without consideration for due process because that is the method of law enforcement which they are accustomed to and respect.

Crime rates

The end of armed hostilities often has the perverse effect of stimulating a crime wave in post-conflict areas.[2] This may be due to a number of factors, including the demobilization of former combatants, the widespread availability of weapons, the absence of economic opportunities, the destruction of the social fabric and the relaxation of wartime controls. Whatever the causes of the upsurge in crime, as its effects are felt there is inevitably a call, internationally and domestically, for the faster deployment of increased numbers of domestic police officers onto the streets. The effect on the transfer of executive authority is twofold. First, the time devoted to training the new local police officers will be seriously circumscribed. Second, the rush to increase their overall numbers can unduly burden the finances of the new law enforcement agency as it may not be balanced by increased tax revenues and their disbursement to law enforcement. As a result, cost savings and trade-offs between salaries, equipment, professional development and institutionalization are required.

---

[2] See, e.g., UN Development Programme, Emergency Response Division, 'Security sector reform assistance in postconflict situations: lessons learned in El Salvador, Guatemala, Haiti, Mozambique, Somalia and Rwanda', 31 Aug. 2001, p. 5; UN Development Programme, *Barometro Centroamericano* (UNDP: San José, Costa Rica, 1997); and Call, C. and Stanley, W., 'Protecting the people: public security choices after civil war', *Global Governance*, no. 7 (2001), pp. 151–72.

The increase in crime often also encourages the development and proliferation of private security companies. These firms may provide a necessary service to local businesses and private individuals given the uncertain law-and-order environment. Unfortunately, however, they can also pose a danger and a direct challenge to a young police agency in that they may originally have been criminal gangs or, conversely, they can easily turn into criminal gangs or become the source from which organized crime arises.[3] Using extortion and other means, they provide security to those who pay for protection and may use the proceeds to expand into other lines of crime. Although street crime may decrease, organized thuggery can grow exponentially.

International involvement and funding

For operational and political reasons the imposition of a 'framework of security' and law and order may be the first item on the agenda of the international community at the start of a peace operation, but it cannot forget that the transition of authority to local structures is the only mechanism by which it can withdraw its law enforcement forces. Furthermore, every action that the international community undertakes in its exercise of executive policing authority will have an effect on the development of the local police service and the way in which the transition takes place. In this sense, the exercise of executive authority and the inevitable transition of those powers to local officials, even though theoretically distinct, are operationally and conceptually intertwined.

Building a local police agency from the ground up takes time. At a very minimum, it can be estimated that the international exercise of executive authority during which the transfer will take place will require a minimum of five years and will be costly. For the international community to maintain its focus and commitment over an extended period of time without suffering donor fatigue is difficult under the best of circumstances. The domestic politics of donor countries and the eruption of fresh international crises will invariably sap the dedication to what is considered a 'now stabilized' but still very fragile post-conflict environment. The financial and human resources

---

[3] See, e.g., 'Security sector reform assistance in postconflict situations' (note 2); and Godnick, W. H., 'La circulacion de armas pequeñas en Centroamerica' [The circulation of small arms in Central America], Paper presented at the Conference on Small and Light Arms in Central America, Stockholm, 18–19 May 1999.

at the disposal of the international community are by definition scarce (in particular, it is difficult for countries to second police officers to UN peace operations) and are quickly channelled to the most prominent current crisis, and projects on which the transfer of executive authority depends often wither on the vine.

A second financial consideration is the mechanism by which the UN conducts its peacekeeping and peace-building work. The transfer of executive authority uneasily straddles the distinction between peace-keeping and peace-building. Operationally, part of the UN funds set aside for the transfer of authority will come from the assessed peace-keeping budget under a Security Council mandate. Typically, these funds will cover the costs of taking on executive authority and the very initial phases in the development of the local police agency. However, most of the monies for the building of the law enforcement service, the other rule-of-law institutions and the transition of executive authority come from voluntary contributions by donor states. These funds may be tied to bilateral agreements between donor countries and the territory in which a peace operation takes place, or they may be funnelled through the UN. Either way, the establishment of the local police agency is heavily dependent on an unsteady stream of contributions, and the civilian police (CivPol) component is compelled to engage in fund-raising and coordinate the activities of donor countries.

Because of these constraints on a UN peace operation, it is highly likely, and very desirable, that before, during and after the transition of policing authority to local officials other international, regional and national organizations step in and assume significant responsibilities. The United Nations Development Programme (UNDP) and the World Bank have ever-increasing roles to play in the institutional development of local police agencies and their 'embedding' in a strong public administration system. Regional organizations should also participate actively as partners with the UN in local police development during or after the transition of authority and the departure of the UN—the primary international mechanism—in order to foster the development of the local police and ensure that the latter can assume their regional responsibilities in addressing the problem of transnational crime. Finally, as pointed out above, bilateral agreements play an invaluable role in facilitating various aspects of the building of the new local law enforcement agency.

III. The timing of the transition

The transfer of executive authority is a long-term proposition. It cannot begin on the first day of the peace operation, but planning the development of the local police agency and the strategic vision of how to accomplish the transfer must begin from 'day one'. It should be the principal objective of all international policing, including those activities that are narrowly focused on the maintenance of law and order. This is not just a question of establishing the conditions for the withdrawal of the international police or acknowledging the intimate connection between the operations of the international police and the development of the local police agency; it is also a management dictum that an organizational unit can only have one overarching goal and that all activities must be geared to furthering its achievement.

The planning, however, cannot remain solely in the hands of the international police because (*a*) it has political and financial ramifications for the future of the territory concerned; (*b*) local political, police and financial actors have to be included in the planning for the envisaged police service because the service must be perceived as theirs and must be shaped to meet local needs, which are best understood by the local actors; and (*c*) a local police service will have an effect on the balance of power between the local political players. The enunciation of the strategic vision must also involve the whole range of international peace personnel.

There is no method of anticipating ahead of time when the actual transfer of authority can start. In reality, this moment will be determined by political considerations and judgements, international and domestic. The start of the transfer will also be affected by the speed with which local governance structures have been established and prove capable of functioning. Nevertheless, international police can and should influence the timing of the transfer on the basis of the academy and in-field training local police officers have received and their ability to absorb and put into practice that training. Again, there is no predetermined level from which to evaluate how much training is sufficient because policing needs will vary from one peace operation to another. For example, the technical skill required to carry out law enforcement in East Timor is not commensurate with the expertise required in Kosovo because of cultural, historical and demographic factors.

A note of caution needs to be sounded here, as it can be anticipated that the international police serving in the peace operation may be reluctant to transfer executive authority to the local police agency as rapidly as may be politically expedient and necessary. This hesitation may have as much to do with their discomfort at no longer possessing executive authority as with their perception of the new local police officers' lack of professional proficiency, their lack of knowledge of the CivPol component's strategic vision, and/or a concomitant deficiency in their training in preparation for the transition. It must be remembered, however, that during the first two years the new local police officers are essentially the equivalent of 'rookie' officers, without experience or seasoning, 'walking a beat' while still in what in most countries would be their probationary period. In this sense, their competence and skills should be evaluated accordingly and expectations lowered to meet operational realities.

IV. Methods of transferring executive authority

Building a law enforcement service is a complex process requiring a range of international and local police and civilian expertise. Conceptually, however, the process of transferring executive authority is relatively straightforward. It appears that there are three 'ideal types' by which the transition can be managed: (*a*) the cocoon–butterfly model; (*b*) the functional model; and (*c*) the geographic model. They are conceptually distinct, with their own logic and strategic visions, but in practice it is more than likely that circumstances will dictate their being 'mixed and matched' to accommodate the operational realities on the ground. Nevertheless, it is important to recognize their differences and to manage the transition accordingly, as one of the three will probably be the predominant one by which the transfer of executive authority takes place.

The starting point for each of the three ideal types is the same—a detailed security assessment of the current and future policing needs of the territory and an evaluation of the educational, technological, infrastructural and cultural realities of the society. What is required is a balancing of security needs with the resources and capital that will be required and available to support their fulfilment, a process that is greater than the sum of its parts and one that requires the active participation of all components of a peace operation, given that the Civ-

Pol component cannot possess the expertise to handle the job on its own. This matching of needs and resources/capital is crucial, for it is difficult to conceive of the police service's long-term survivability if its structure, organization and force projection do not correspond to societal needs and cannot be adequately supported or resourced.[4] It must be acknowledged, however, that conditions change and that the security requirements that exist during the first year of a peace operation may not be the same as those that exist in subsequent years. For this reason the initial security assessment must be able to project future needs so that the burgeoning domestic police service is not overhauled before it is even officially inaugurated.

Once needs have been matched with resources/capital, the blueprint of the new local police service can be revised and finalized. Because the composition and control of the new local police service will inevitably affect the political balance of power, it is preferable for the peace accords that ended the armed conflict to set down the basic outlines of what the new local police service will look like. This is especially important regarding the demographic composition of the new law enforcement agency. Admittedly this will be difficult to achieve in each and every case, but past experience indicates that it is highly advisable to do so.[5] If the peace accords do not lay down the basic parameters, including the constitutional foundation and structure of the police, its relation to the military, its total permissible human resource complement and its demographic composition, then it is essential that local political leaders be intimately involved at the very start of the peace operation in the drafting of the blueprint to ensure the service's legitimacy and acceptance. What this means in practice is that local law enforcement, political and civil society representatives—elected or otherwise—must be included in all stages of the

---

[4] Judging from interviews conducted by the author it appears that neither a comprehensive security assessment nor a resource/capital evaluation was carried out by either UNMIK or UNTAET. A perusal of official UN documents suggests that the interview findings are accurate.

[5] The El Salvador and Guatemala experiences are particularly instructive on the need for police advice and expertise during peace negotiations. Bosnia and Herzegovina is another case in point given the time it took for the Republika Srpska to agree to the restructuring of its police service and the significant disparities between its Framework Agreement signed with the United Nations in 1998 and that signed by the Federation of Bosnia and Herzegovina in 1996, the Bonn–Petersberg Agreement. The fact that as of Dec. 2001 very few, if any, of the demographic 'benchmarks' in either agreement had been reached only confirms the need to have such commitments embedded in the original peace accords.

planning and development of the local police service from the very first days of the peace operation.[6]

The drafting of the police service's blueprint can be broken down into discrete elements: (a) strategic vision; (b) composition—number of officers, rank and hierarchy, demographic distribution of manpower and so on; (c) structure—ministry, regional, district, local, chains of command, number of officers in selected police disciplines and so on; (d) financial foundation—budgets; and (e) administrative support—public administration.[7] Without question, this process will be time-consuming, and because of its wide-ranging scope it needs, once again, to involve all the elements of a peace operation, given that CivPol components traditionally do not have political, financial or public administration expertise within their ranks.[8] This process must begin quickly and be systematic and detailed. It is difficult to envisage the successful development of the local police service without a well-conceived blueprint, to say nothing about its long-term sustainability.

The last step that is common to all three 'ideal-type' approaches is the recruitment and selection of candidates for service in the new law enforcement agency, the establishment of a police academy and curri-culum, and the in-field training programme for the new graduates of the academy. Along with the determination of the local police ser-vice's rank structure, this last step is perhaps the easiest task in the creation of a local police service as it focuses exclusively on the pro-fessional training of the individual police officer. It is also the one at which the DPKO is most proficient.

---

[6] There may be many different methods of bringing local police and political and civil leaders 'on board', depending on the particular circumstances of the peace operation, includ-ing formal incorporation into the CivPol component of the peace operation, political consulta-tions, quiet, private negotiations, town hall meetings, conferences and public opinion surveys, but the way in which local partners are brought into the planning and development process is less important than the fact that they are closely involved.

[7] Judging from interviews conducted by the author it appears that neither UNMIK nor UNTAET drafted an all-encompassing blueprint. In the case of UNTAET, as of Jan. 2002 it seems that such a document still did not exist. A perusal of official UN documents supports this finding.

[8] At the time of writing (Jan. 2002), there were no experienced political, financial or public administration experts serving in the UNMIK or UNTAET CivPol components. The same could be said for the UN Mission in Bosnia and Herzegovina (UNMIBH), the UN Mission in Sierra Leone (UNAMSIL) and the UN Observer Mission in the Democratic Republic of the Congo (MONUC) operations. Nor are there any serving in New York in the Civilian Police Division of the DPKO. However, the DPKO 100-person on-call roster proposal does include these experts for rapid deployment at the start-up of future CivPol peace operations, and it is expected that the staffing tables of CivPol components will be modified accordingly.

Cocoon–butterfly

As the name suggests, this ideal type is premised upon building the new domestic police service in embryonic form and 'growing' it within the confines and safety of the international police force until such time as it is able to take flight on its own and assume full responsibility for law and order. Growing the domestic police service within the structure of the CivPol component means that each and every unit, office and department of the indigenous agency takes shape inside the comparable CivPol unit, office or department. Conceptually, the CivPol police commissioner will have his or her local counterpart, as will the commissioner's legal adviser, spokesperson, and policy and planning staff. The CivPol operations, criminal investigations, crowd control, personnel and internal affairs departments, and others, will all be mirrored by local ones. If particular units do not exist within the CivPol component—for example, finance, procurement, facilities management or forensics—special arrangements will be required so that the necessary local capacities are created, cultivated and developed in an appropriate and timely manner.

As the local law enforcement agency grows there will be a point in time when it can be said that two parallel police organizations coexist within one body. It is then that the protective CivPol sheathing can be shed and the local police service officially inaugurated. As mentioned above, there is a caveat as to whether the overall public administration and political apparatus in the territory in question is operational at roughly the same time as that of the police service. The police cannot be the first public service to be de-internationalized because the police do not and cannot operate in a vacuum. A civil service must be functional, tax revenues must be collected and disbursed and, most importantly, a political system must be in place to which the police report and which has oversight of them.

Of the three ideal types the cocoon–butterfly option is the most comprehensive and organizationally sound in the sense that an entire agency is formed and developed step by step as an organic whole. Discrepancies and disparities between organizational units within the local law enforcement agency will be minimized and the full range of polices, procedures and processes coordinated. However, there are three difficulties.

First, the international community perhaps retains full executive authority longer with this ideal type of transition than with the others, as the incubation period will be long. Consequently, there may be domestic political pressures to speed up the process as it pertains to one or more operational police units. Such political realities may be difficult to manage and it is likely that a high degree of flexibility in approach will be required.

Second, there is a severe logical, cultural and practical disjuncture in the cocoon–butterfly option. Since the local police service is incubated within the body of the CivPol component during the period when executive authority is exercised by the international community, the local service will be deeply influenced by, if not inevitably mirror, the structures and practices of its host organism. However, the international police component is a foreign structure in terms of organization, procedure and personnel. No matter how responsive it is to local needs, it cannot adapt entirely to local mores, customs and traditions. It would therefore be a mistake for the local police service to adopt the CivPol model. It may be argued that the CivPol structure and operations can be systematically redesigned to meet the needs of the emerging local police service but, given the number of countries from which CivPol officers are drawn, it is highly doubtful whether this can be achieved.

Third, the cocoon–butterfly model assumes that the CivPol component is a relatively cohesive, coherent and consistent 'host organism', but this may not be so. The rapid change in the leadership not only of CivPol components but of peace operations themselves undermines the notion of a consistent host organism: each change of leadership always results in significant policy alterations. The frequent rotation of CivPol personnel also weakens the component's ability to maintain the coherence and cohesiveness that the model assumes and requires.

Functional

Unlike the cocoon–butterfly technique, the functional model breaks down a law enforcement agency into its component parts and disciplines. Each unit, office and department is perceived as a discrete whole within a larger organization and its development proceeds according to its own logic and requirements. The reintroduction of a local police patrol capacity occurs independently from that of the indigenous crime investigation unit, crowd control squad or police budgeting and accounting office.

The benefit and advantages of this approach are straightforward. Unlike the cocoon–butterfly option, it permits great flexibility and variation. The need to coordinate the establishment of the local police service with that of other criminal justice, public administration and political institutions is reduced because local law enforcement can come on-line piecemeal while the international community may still retain overall executive and transitional authority, for instance, in the judiciary or the tax authorities. Furthermore, the training needs of the various police disciplines and capacities differ. It takes significantly longer, for example, to develop a forensics or internal affairs unit than to develop a traffic department. In fact, there may be a logical training sequence in the creation of a new police service, beginning with the traffic and uniformed departments, which explicitly favours the functional approach. All local police officers are trained in basic policing skills and rotated through these first two disciplines (assuming, of course, a security need for a traffic capacity). Those local police officers who exhibit greater aptitude and skills can then be given advanced courses in these disciplines along with initial management education. Bit by bit, operational and command authority for these disciplines can be transferred to local police personnel while the CivPol component retains overall executive authority. If and when such a limited transfer of policing powers is successful, those local officers who have proved their worth can be moved to other disciplines and given additional training, thereby slowly but progressively expanding their professional abilities at the same time as the local police service's institutional competencies are grown.

Because of its inherently piecemeal approach, the functional option has two other very desirable advantages. First, it can encourage the shaping of each police organization unit according to the beliefs, mores and practices of the local culture. As there is no 'one size fits all' technique borrowed from a foreign organization, adaptation to the local environment can be encouraged and flower. Second, the functional approach is more likely to take into account the fact that the local law enforcement agency, for operational or financial (sustainability) reasons, may not require certain police disciplines either 'upfront' or down the line. Given its step-by-step methodology, the functional approach can put off the introduction of these disciplines until the foreseeable security situation demands them and the financial structure of society and the government can reasonably support them. For example, it may be not only more cost-effective to outsource advanced forensic investigations to a foreign organization or country, but also more efficacious operationally with respect to solving specific crimes. From this perspective, therefore, the functional approach may be the most operationally sound and cost-effective option.

There are, however, certain drawbacks.

First, political imperatives may necessitate the development of particular police disciplines, such as close protection and crowd control, before training can be completed and financial resources are in place. It may even be the case that some police disciplines are not needed from a security perspective but are called for nevertheless by international and local political leaders. Because of the inherently political and non-linear nature of peace operations, such necessities must be acknowledged, accepted and acted upon.

Second, because of its progressive and gradual technique, the functional approach is time-consuming. Political realities, however, may not permit the luxury of time.

Third, the decision may have been made that the new local police agency will incorporate into its ranks officers who have had extensive previous experience. Their professional development may well proceed faster than the indigenous law enforcement organization can be grown. It would be inappropriate to hold their professional development hostage to purely organizational considerations, and it may be best to integrate them directly into the CivPol component at a level commensurate with their skills and experience.

Finally, unless it is tightly controlled the functional approach may produce dislocations between police disciplines because of the constant changes in the CivPol personnel who train the local police officers. It is possible, for example, for the uniformed department to have been exposed to a policing model primarily derived from a particular policing tradition while the internal affairs unit, at a later date, is taught a significantly different technique based on another policing practice. This is not to say that one or another policing tradition is better or worse than another, but that there must be consistency and relative uniformity in the introduction of policing styles and practices in the development of the local law enforcement agency.

Geographic

The third approach to building a local police service and transferring executive authority to it is the geographic approach. This tactic aims to transfer policing powers in selected areas of the territory under transitional administration one by one in a patchwork process. Sites for the transfer of executive authority are chosen for their low incidence of crime or low levels of political tension and ethnic, religious, tribal or other competition that may have originally triggered conflict. Other variables that may be taken into account in determining the geographic sequence of the transfer of authority are (a) the ability of the international community to control the area in question, (b) the development of local political structures to ensure balance in the creation of local governance, and (c) political agreement by the local parties on the suitability of chosen sites.

The advantage of this method of transferring authority lies in its site-specific approach. The initial geographic areas are selected precisely to maximize the chances of a successful transfer. It can be hypothesized that those areas are likely to be more rather than less remote, thinly populated and relatively small. The local officers will therefore learn how to conduct and manage their own operations under favourable conditions. Those officials and units which succeed and exhibit technical proficiency and managerial talent can graduate from one site to the next, with each site being of increased complexity and difficulty, and their abilities can thus be honed in a gradual and progressive way.

The disadvantages of this approach are numerous. First, it presupposes that at each site when executive authority is transferred the local police will possess the full range of capabilities, units and equipment required to enforce law and order—not only uniformed, criminal investigation and traffic departments but also, if necessary, crowd control, internal affairs, and financial, accounting and facility maintenance units. To establish and equip comprehensive mini-police agencies one by one may not be practical or feasible given the inevitable resource constraints and the disparities in the length of training time required for different police disciplines. It may not, for instance, be practical to wait for the transfer of authority for uniformed policing until an internal affairs unit is fully operational. Furthermore, it may be politically impossible to do so. Second, all the disadvantages of the cocoon–butterfly model also apply to the geographic model. Finally, the most pressing obstacle may be the inability to develop parallel local criminal justice, public administration and governance structures on a piecemeal basis. In fact, it is very probable that this will be operationally, structurally and legally impossible.

V. Field experience: Kosovo and East Timor

At the time of writing (January 2002), neither the Kosovo nor the East Timor peace operation has progressed sufficiently far down the road to transferring executive authority for constructive comment on the successful evolution of their transitions to be possible. In neither operation is official documentation available outlining the method by which the peace operation intends to transfer police authority. General tendencies can be identified, but not with any precision. Furthermore, in both cases it seems that the final composition and structure of the respective local law enforcement agencies that the international community is building remain fundamentally in flux. Although the rank and hierarchical structure of the respective local police services has been established and is developing according to plan, there seems to be little agreement on what the East Timorese or Kosovo police service will look like regarding final total complement of local police officers, the numbers of officers who will work in each law enforcement discipline or where they will ultimately be stationed.[9]

This underlying lack of agreement may be due to political uncertainty, the lack of a parallel and comparable development in the other branches of the criminal justice system and the fragility of the supporting public administration infrastructure. It can, however, also be attributed to the lack in either operation of comprehensive financial analyses of the level and type of public revenues for law enforcement that will be sustainable in the long run. As a result it is very possible, if not highly likely, that both domestic law enforcement agencies will have to be restructured and downsized in the next few years while the transfer of authority takes place. It is thus highly problematic to discuss with any specificity the eventual transfer of executive authority from the international to domestic officials.

---

[9] E.g., in Dec. 2001 the author was informed by an UNTAET police planner that one 'cannot tell as of today how many East Timorese will be in any single police discipline'.

Nevertheless, extensive interviews conducted by the author through-out 2001 suggest that it is possible to discern the broad contours of the peace operations' initial approach to the issue of the transfer of authority. Although both operations are selecting elements of all three approaches, mixing and matching them to meet local conditions, it seems that they have, at least initially, stressed different options. At first, the East Timor mission appeared to emphasize the cocoon–butterfly model, but it has now tilted to a more functional strategy. The Kosovo operation, on the other hand, may be adopting a more geographic technique in its transfer of executive authority.

Kosovo

The sensitive ethnic balance that must be maintained in the territory complicates the management of the Kosovo transition of executive authority, as do the unresolved final political status of the territory and the fact that the total number of police officers expected to serve in what will be the Kosovo Police Service (KPS) is continually being increased because of persisting instability in the security situation. It is more than challenging to plan a transition when the final target is in continual flux. Further challenges arise given the slow progress in establishing an impartial, independent and multi-ethnic judiciary. Nevertheless, as in East Timor, the training of local police officers has progressed well, both in terms of overall numbers and in increasing the percentage of first-line and middle-level supervisors serving in the local law enforcement agency. Some senior appointments have been made at the colonel and lieutenant-colonel levels, and these officers 'shadow' their UNMIK colleagues to learn and refine their trade.

Faced with these profound uncertainties and challenges, in August 2001 the head of the KPS admitted that its formation was only in a 'nascent stage'. At that time, he stated that his intention was to begin to turn over the in-field training of recently qualified officers to local Kosovo trainers, despite severe opposition. He anticipated that this 'experiment', as he called it, could begin at the earliest by December 2001. Simultaneously, advanced courses will be given to KPS officers in forensics, organized crime, criminal investigations, community policing and other specialized police disciplines. Finally, adopting the geographic model, the head of the KPS claimed that he wanted to initiate the actual transition of executive authority within 18 months by turning over control of a local police station, but that nothing had been definitively decided. It is currently anticipated that the first local police station will be turned over to the KPS in or before December 2002. If all proceeds well, it can be expected that command of additional police stations will be handed over to the KPS, although no precise figures are currently available.[10]

Unfortunately, as in the East Timor case, there may not be sufficient funds to support the development of the KPS as currently configured, let alone a police service of ever-increasing numbers. The Kosovo Government does not have the public monies to sustain local KPS police operations, let alone the back-office support activities that will be required.[11] For example, as one source claimed, the offices and stations from which the KPS currently operates are 'decrepit, anti-quated and inadequate' but as there are 'almost no' funds available to upgrade them little can be done to improve the situation.[12]

Once again, because of the absence of a comprehensive financial analysis of the security situation it is feared that there will be very limited monies for the maintenance of police equipment, professional development and other needs not directly related to the salaries of police officers and the supply of very basic police equipment. For instance, it is alleged that, at this point in time, there are not sufficient funds available to equip, train and deploy a KPS special unit for high-risk operations. A very simple but telling example makes the case: KPS officers are provided with four sets of uniforms, two for winter and two for summer, but it is widely acknowledged this is insufficient, especially as no replacement uniforms are furnished and salaries are too low for the officers to buy their own. Without adequate funding for the KPS, the mechanisms by which the transfer of executive authority is realized are less relevant than the law enforcement agency that is left behind.

East Timor

On two separate visits to East Timor in 2001, the author was told that the UNTAET CivPol component would be 'Timorized'—East Timorese police officers would be 'co-located' with international police

---

[10] Author's interviews with senior UNMIK police staff, Aug. 2001.
[11] Author's interviews with a senior public administration official in UNMIK, Aug. 2001.
[12] Author's interviews with senior UNMIK police staff, Aug. and Dec. 2001.

officers in each operational and functional civilian police unit.[13] Following the cocoon–butterfly approach, the intention appeared to be that the local police would 'mirror' the structure, functions and activities of the international police from top to bottom. As the head of the East Timor Police Service (ETPS) indicated, the technique would allow the East Timorese to 'take ownership' of the international police organization in an 'office by office' manner while learning from and absorbing the international police's expertise.[14] Under this plan it was envisaged that the ETPS would include units for general duties, investigations, internal affairs, rapid response, marine, VIP close protection, criminal intelligence and vulnerable persons.

In the summer of 2001, in discussions with the ETPS, certain conceptual weaknesses in the cocoon–butterfly model became apparent. For example, because the local police service was designed to mirror the UNTAET CivPol component, little planning was done with regard to those managerial and administrative areas that lay outside the purview of the CivPol component—budgeting, procurement, logistics, facilities maintenance, asset management and human resource planning. Specifically, the author was told in December 2001 that 'virtually nothing' had been done to develop the police's non-sworn civil service staff. There have also been difficulties as a result of the disjuncture between the development of the police and the difficulty in preparing, drafting and passing the necessary supporting national legislation. The author was told that the draft police law establishing the ETPS took almost a year to be enacted and that East Timorese police officers had already been exercising policing powers prior to its final passage.[15]

Consequently, in the second half of 2001 the original model was modified and new plans devised. Even though East Timorese police officers are now co-located throughout the UNTAET CivPol component, the headquarters staff being the only exception, the plans call for selected functional policing disciplines to be turned over to local control one at a time. For instance, in Dili the East Timorese police are gradually being given responsibility for security in the harbour, providing close protection to selected domestic political leaders, and traffic control, and East Timorese criminal investigators are handling

[13] Author's interviews with the head of the East Timorese Police Unit, the unit responsible for the development of the ETPS, Feb. and July 2001.

[14] Author's interview with the head of the ETPS, Feb. 2001.

[15] Author's interviews with senior UNTAET civilian and police staff, Feb. 2001.

most, if not all, crimes committed by Timorese against Timorese. Local trainers have also begun to work extensively in the East Timorese police academy. Next on the list will be airport security and a specialized rapid response unit for crowd control.

At the same time, borrowing from the geographic approach, it is expected that executive authority will be transferred at the local police station level as well. A timetable exists for the progressive handover of authority taking into account such factors as demographic distribution, criminal activity, logistical access and material requirements.[16] Simultaneously, however, police stations will have to be consolidated and their operations reassessed because of lack of financial resources. It was also made clear that the establishment of the local judiciary and the overall public administration framework is lagging badly behind that of the police, and that this uneven development will have severe repercussions for the solidification of an effective criminal justice system. For example, it was reported that there is no law or regulation in existence for developing an internal affairs department within the ETPS, thus hampering the institutionalization of one of the more central elements of any police service.

This combined financial and governance 'squeeze' on the emerging domestic law enforcement agency calls into question how the transfer of executive authority will take place and what the resulting East Timorese police will look like. It was originally anticipated that the local police agency would comprise 2400–3000 officers, but even the lower number may be financially unsustainable. Not only will the local police have to be 'immediately downsized', as a senior UNTAET police planner claimed, but the total number and operations of local police stations will have to be 'swiftly reconfigured' because of the lack of funds. Furthermore, there will be a serious lack of money for the maintenance and repair of police equipment, communications systems and essential buildings. The professional development and in-service training of local police officers will have to be curtailed or made 'wholly dependent' on external resources such as bilateral relationships with donor countries. Finally, it is anticipated that there will be up to 400 non-sworn support staff positions but very little has been done to establish these 'back-office functions', to say nothing of the financial wherewithal to pay for these essential activities.

---

[16] Author's interviews with senior UNTAET police staff, July and Dec. 2001.

'Everything depends on money' and the 'local police cannot even afford the bare necessities'.[17]

VI. Conclusions

Few, if any, conclusions can be reached from the exceedingly limited practical experience in transferring executive authority from a United Nations police service to a local law enforcement agency. The initial steps in the transition process in Kosovo and East Timor suggest that no one approach will suffice. Rather a 'mix and match' strategy is most probably the most effective and efficient method of transferring authority. Nevertheless, it appears that the 'functional' approach may be the one which gains dominance because of the necessity to provide rudimentary law and order functions as quickly as possible, not just to meet political imperatives but because that is the natural progression in the training of police officers.

There is, however, a more important conclusion. Insufficient attention has been paid to the financial sustainability of local police services after executive authority has been transferred to them. As a result, the police services that will be left behind by the international community may be institutionally fragile, may find it difficult to support their law enforcement operations administratively or managerially, and may be less than able to develop professionally and limited in their capacity to maintain their equipment and buildings. To survive they may have to depend on regional and bilateral assistance programmes for financing and professional development, and the outsourcing of certain police disciplines such as forensic investigations.

The law enforcement personnel, sworn and non-sworn, are public servants and the institutions in which they serve must be sustained through public monies. After an extended period of conflict there may be few tax revenue generation possibilities with which to fund government activities, including law enforcement. This factor must be taken into account at the outset of the international effort to build a new local police service rather than at the back end, as seems to have been the case in Kosovo and East Timor. Ultimately, these financial considerations will have a significant, if not determining, role in moulding the type and quality of services local police agencies can provide.

---

[17] Author's interview with a senior member of UNTAET's CivPol component, Dec. 2001.

8. Conclusions

Renata Dwan

That the Kosovo and East Timor operations remain the only two instances of executive policing in UN peace operations is, for many, proof that they are unique and that little comparison is possible with other types of international police mission. The experience of both thus far amply demonstrates the enormous difficulties of practical international law enforcement. According to this perspective, the lessons of the two operations make executive policing less, rather than more, likely in the future. Some observers would conclude that it is, therefore, a subject of limited policy relevance. This book testifies to the opposite, for two basic reasons.

I. Lessons for executive policing

First, however singular the two cases are, neither instance of executive policing shows signs of coming to an end in the near future. Reflecting about such missions, what they entail and how they can be better carried out in the future is thus an important task for the research community.

1. The six chapters in this volume show convincingly how international law enforcement in both Kosovo and East Timor was and continues to be implemented in an ad hoc manner. There was little strategic thinking in 1999 on how executive policing might be conceived or implemented and, in the absence of any framework, international police personnel inevitably relied on a mixture of standard UN civilian police (CivPol) practice and their personal policing experience. The result in many instances, as Colette Rausch and Eirin Mobekk point out, was at best confusion and at worst failure. The speed with which the two transitional administrations were launched may explain the lack of planning, but cannot justify the continuation of ad hoc approaches to executive policing.

As Eric Scheye's contribution illustrates, each different phase of the peace-building process makes new demands on the executive policing operation, for which additional advance thinking and planning is required.

2. This volume affirms the enormity of the challenge of executive policing. None of the authors shirks the fact of the sheer difficulty of it, and running through the book is the implicit suggestion that international law enforcement should be approached with caution. Rausch argues that the establishment and widespread communication of a clear legal framework is a prerequisite to any practical law enforcement by an international police presence. Her view is repeatedly echoed in the examinations that follow of the type of policing to be undertaken and police–military relations in executive policing operations. This position would suggest the merit of the proposal raised in the Brahimi Report and elsewhere, that UN 'model codes' or 'justice packages' be developed for temporary use by the international community in crisis situations.[1] More attention could also be given to the dissemination of and instruction in applicable law to newly-deployed international police as well as to local law enforcement personnel.

3. A third theme that emerges from consideration of the difficulties involved is the need for clear priorities to be set. International actors and local populations must accept that international policing in a post-conflict situation will be, of necessity, limited in the number of objectives it can successfully achieve and priorities must therefore be established. Michael J. Dziedzic offers one approach to agenda-setting and demonstrates how the focus of international police efforts can evolve as a peace operation progresses. Mobekk's chapter drives home the point that 'normal' policing strategies are not possible in an abnormal policing context. Yet, as all the chapters illustrate, such prioritization is extremely difficult.

Concentrating on one aspect of policing (e.g., public order) at the expense of a less explosive one (e.g., public outreach) may undermine local popular support for the international police presence, which is the ultimate basis on which the legitimacy of executive policing rests. A strategy which focuses on counter-terrorist activity and on building local capacities for this might neglect other aspects of policing and system building which are important for the protection of innocent citizens and civil liberties. This type of narrowly focused approach

---

[1] United Nations, Report of the Panel on United Nations Peace Operations, UN document A/55/305, S/2000/809, 21 Aug. 2000 (the Brahimi Report). See also Austin, R., 'A legal framework for a democratic public order system' in Institute of Policy Studies (IPS) and United Nations Institute for Training and Research (UNITAR), *The Role and Functions of Civilian Police in United Nations Peacekeeping Operations: Debriefing and Lessons* (Kluwer Law International: London, 1996), pp. 129–34.

may also militate against the effectiveness of international policing, not least if areas such as the fight against organized crime or local police training are neglected. Finally, it may work against the sustainability of local police reform by failing to address transformation from the bottom up.

4. Some of the authors suggest that one way around this is to think in strategic terms of operational phases and to focus on the appropriate policing tasks for each one. All point to the need for more thinking on what these tasks might be at any one stage, what they require in terms of resources, and how they might be implemented. Both Annika S. Hansen and Scheye caution, however, against rigid 'phaseology' and show that the stages of a peace operation overlap, are prone to temporary setbacks and vary. One aspect of a police operation—for example, the number of local police cadets—may improve exponentially while another—for example, the proportion of solved crimes—may remain stagnant. A much more complex picture of the different phases of a peace operation is therefore required.

5. All six authors are clear that one key to managing this complexity is greater interaction and coordination between the police element of a peace operation and its military, judicial and human rights elements. Formal divisions of labour between them only go part of the way towards enabling an integrated rule-of-law approach and effective international law enforcement. Frameworks of communication and coordination are required at the strategic and operational levels if police–military and police–judiciary cooperation is to be institutionalized. As Hansen hints, this is as much a cultural as a structural challenge. Domestic police cultures, in Western democracies at least, tend to be relatively insular and often suspicious of close contact with the military, while the judiciary is often perceived as a related but separate element of the rule of law. Multifunctional team approaches are required for international law enforcement and are one of the most important avenues for further research and practical development.

6. Another important strand for successful executive policing is interaction with the local authorities and population. Not only, as Robert Perito and Scheye point out, is it a condition of ending international law enforcement operations; it is also vital for the practice of executive policing. Mobekk notes that this element of peace operations is sometimes neglected: as a consequence, international policing practices may fail to adequately address the needs and concerns of the

society in question. Given the intensity with which the police component of a peace operation interacts with the local population, the active involvement of local actors is a crucial element for successful executive policing. This represents another area for future research.

II. Legacies of executive policing

A second reason why executive policing is here to stay is the influence it will have on future international policing in peace operations, executive or not.

1. The Kosovo and East Timor police operations have put the final nail in the coffin of the SMART concept with its emphasis on police monitoring and training as a discrete function of a peace operation.[2] International policing is increasingly recognized as a project of reform and restructuring: its goal is the fundamental and enduring transformation of a society.

2. The implication of this wider concept, as every author points out, is that a more comprehensive and holistic approach to the rule of law is needed. Police reform must be located within this wider framework and developed in close partnership with its political, military, social, judicial and penal elements. Better integration of the different components of peace operations is now a principal concern for the UN and regional organizations in their efforts to develop peacekeeping and peace-building capacities.

3. This new emphasis, as the Kosovo and East Timor experiences have borne out, highlights the political nature of international policing. Police reform and training are not, as they tended to be portrayed in the past, an exercise in the transfer of technical skills but, as Scheye argues, a political project that changes power relationships in the society in question. The implication of this, for Dziedzic, is that international peace operations must address local political will for peaceful change and must actively tackle those in the society that oppose this process. Future international policing operations are likely to engage more energetically than in the past with the political reform process of the society in which they operate.

4. The experience of executive policing since 1999 has also confirmed the long-term nature of peace-building. All the authors in this

---

[2] See chapter 1 in this volume.

volume stress the length of time required for sustainable transformation and emphasize the structural and institutional assistance components of international policing. Policing in UN peace operations cannot be isolated within the framework of peacekeeping; indeed, actors such as the United Nations Development Programme (UNDP) which focus on peace-building are now becoming more engaged in police reform. Regional organizations, such as the European Union (EU) and the Organization for Security and Co-operation in Europe (OSCE), have acknowledged this longer-term approach and must now tackle the resource consequences of undertaking policing commitments.[3]

The international police resources Kosovo and East Timor will continue to require make it extremely unlikely that more executive police operations will be undertaken in the immediate future. The emerging lessons of both operations are likely to make international organizations and their member states more, rather than less, hesitant about negotiating the inescapable political, financial and legal challenges of executive policing. Finally, the contexts of Kosovo and East Timor—with small territories and broad international support for their substantial autonomy and/or independence—are not likely to be replicated in the near future. For these reasons, at least, executive policing may not be initiated again in the short term, regardless of whether there is a need or demand for international law enforcement. However, the effects of its two instances will be manifested in the way future police work is carried out in peace operations as diverse as those in Afghanistan, the Democratic Republic of the Congo and Sierra Leone.

It is too early for conclusive lessons to be drawn from the Kosovo and East Timor experiences. As detailed studies emerge, international policy makers, police and researchers will be able to build a more comprehensive picture of the strategies and tools of executive policing to shape future police operations, be they executive or, as is more likely, extensive reform and restructuring missions. Far from being the end, the cases of Kosovo and East Timor represent the start of fundamental thinking on international policing for peace.

---

[3] See, e.g., European Union, Police Capabilities Commitment Conference, 'Declaration', Brussels, 19 Nov. 2001, document 14197/2001.

Appendix A. UN Security Council resolutions 1244 and 1272

UN Security Council Resolution 1244 (1999)

10 June 1999

Excerpts

The Security Council,

Bearing in mind the purposes and principles of the Charter of the United Nations, and the primary responsibility of the Security Council for the maintenance of international peace and security,

Recalling its resolutions 1160 (1998) of 31 March 1998, 1199 (1998) of 23 September 1998, 1203 (1998) of 24 October 1998 and 1239 (1999) of 14 May 1999,

Regretting that there has not been full compliance with the requirements of these resolutions,

Determined to resolve the grave humanitarian situation in Kosovo, Federal Republic of Yugoslavia, and to provide for the safe and free return of all refugees and displaced persons to their homes,

. . .

Reaffirming the right of all refugees and displaced persons to return to their homes in safety,

Recalling the jurisdiction and the mandate of the International Tribunal for the Former Yugoslavia,

Welcoming the general principles on a political solution to the Kosovo crisis adopted on 6 May 1999 (S/1999/516, annex 1 to this resolution) and welcoming also the acceptance by the Federal Republic of Yugoslavia of the principles set forth in points 1 to 9 of the paper presented in Belgrade on 2 June 1999 (S/1999/649, annex 2 to this resolution), and the Federal Republic of Yugoslavia's agreement to that paper,

Reaffirming the commitment of all Member States to the sovereignty and territorial integrity of the Federal Republic of Yugoslavia and the other States of the region, as set out in the Helsinki Final Act and annex 2,

Reaffirming the call in previous resolutions for substantial autonomy and meaningful self-administration for Kosovo,

Determining that the situation in the region continues to constitute a threat to international peace and security,

Determined to ensure the safety and security of international personnel and the implementation by all concerned of their responsibilities under the present resolution, and *acting* for these purposes under Chapter VII of the Charter of the United Nations,

1. *Decides* that a political solution to the Kosovo crisis shall be based on the general principles in annex 1 and as further elaborated in the principles and other required elements in annex 2;

2. *Welcomes* the acceptance by the Federal Republic of Yugoslavia of the principles and other required elements referred to in paragraph 1 above, and *demands* the full cooperation of the Federal Republic of Yugoslavia in their rapid implementation;

3. *Demands* in particular that the Federal Republic of Yugoslavia put an immediate and verifiable end to violence and repression in Kosovo, and begin and

complete verifiable phased withdrawal from Kosovo of all military, police and paramilitary forces according to a rapid timetable, with which the deployment of the international security presence in Kosovo will be synchronized;

4. *Confirms* that after the withdrawal an agreed number of Yugoslav and Serb military and police personnel will be permitted to return to Kosovo to perform the functions in accordance with annex 2;

5. *Decides* on the deployment in Kosovo, under United Nations auspices, of international civil and security presences, with appropriate equipment and personnel as required, and welcomes the agreement of the Federal Republic of Yugoslavia to such presences;

6. *Requests* the Secretary-General to appoint, in consultation with the Security Council, a Special Representative to control the implementation of the international civil presence, and *further requests* the Secretary-General to instruct his Special Representative to coordinate closely with the international security presence to ensure that both presences operate towards the same goals and in a mutually supportive manner;

7. *Authorizes* Member States and relevant international organizations to establish the international security presence in Kosovo as set out in point 4 of annex 2 with all necessary means to fulfil its responsibilities under paragraph 9 below;

8. *Affirms* the need for the rapid early deployment of effective international civil and security presences to Kosovo, and *demands* that the parties cooperate fully in their deployment;

9. *Decides* that the responsibilities of the international security presence to be deployed and acting in Kosovo will include:

(*a*) Deterring renewed hostilities, maintaining and where necessary enforcing a ceasefire, and ensuring the withdrawal and preventing the return into Kosovo of Federal and Republic military, police and paramilitary forces, except as provided in point 6 of annex 2;

(*b*) Demilitarizing the Kosovo Liberation Army (KLA) and other armed Kosovo Albanian groups as required in paragraph 15 below;

(*c*) Establishing a secure environment in which refugees and displaced persons can return home in safety, the international civil presence can operate, a transitional administration can be established, and humanitarian aid can be delivered;

(*d*) Ensuring public safety and order until the international civil presence can take responsibility for this task;

(*e*) Supervising demining until the international civil presence can, as appropriate, take over responsibility for this task;

(*f*) Supporting, as appropriate, and coordinating closely with the work of the international civil presence;

(*g*) Conducting border monitoring duties as required;

(*h*) Ensuring the protection and freedom of movement of itself, the international civil presence, and other international organizations;

10. *Authorizes* the Secretary-General, with the assistance of relevant international organizations, to establish an international civil presence in Kosovo in order to provide an interim administration for Kosovo under which the people of Kosovo can enjoy substantial autonomy within the Federal Republic of Yugoslavia, and which will provide transitional administration while establishing and overseeing the development of provisional democratic self-governing

institutions to ensure conditions for a peaceful and normal life for all inhabitants of Kosovo;

11. *Decides* that the main responsibilities of the international civil presence will include:

(*a*) Promoting the establishment, pending a final settlement, of substantial autonomy and self-government in Kosovo, taking full account of annex 2 and of the Rambouillet accords (S/1999/648);

(*b*) Performing basic civilian administrative functions where and as long as required;

(*c*) Organizing and overseeing the development of provisional institutions for democratic and autonomous self-government pending a political settlement, including the holding of elections;

(*d*) Transferring, as these institutions are established, its administrative responsibilities while overseeing and supporting the consolidation of Kosovo's local provisional institutions and other peace-building activities;

(*e*) Facilitating a political process designed to determine Kosovo's future status, taking into account the Rambouillet accords (S/1999/648);

(*f*) In a final stage, overseeing the transfer of authority from Kosovo's provisional institutions to institutions established under a political settlement;

(*g*) Supporting the reconstruction of key infrastructure and other economic reconstruction;

(*h*) Supporting, in coordination with international humanitarian organizations, humanitarian and disaster relief aid;

(*i*) Maintaining civil law and order, including establishing local police forces and meanwhile through the deployment of international police personnel to serve in Kosovo;

(*j*) Protecting and promoting human rights;

(*k*) Assuring the safe and unimpeded return of all refugees and displaced persons to their homes in Kosovo;

12. *Emphasizes* the need for coordinated humanitarian relief operations, and for the Federal Republic of Yugoslavia to allow unimpeded access to Kosovo by humanitarian aid organizations . . .

. . .

19. *Decides* that the international civil and security presences are established for an initial period of 12 months, to continue thereafter unless the Security Council decides otherwise;

. . .

[Annexes 1 and 2 not reproduced here.]

Source: UN Security Council Resolution 1244, 10 June 1999, available on the UN Internet site at <http://www.un.org/Docs/scres/1999/sc99.htm>.

UN Security Council Resolution 1272

25 October 1999

Excerpts

The Security Council,

Recalling its previous resolutions and the statements of its President on the situation in East Timor, in particular resolutions 384 (1975) of 22 December 1975, 389 (1976) of 22 April 1976, 1236 (1999) of 7 May 1999, 1246 (1999) of 11 June 1999, 1262 (1999) of 27 August 1999 and 1264 (1999) of 15 September 1999,

...

Reiterating its welcome for the successful conduct of the popular consultation of the East Timorese people of 30 August 1999, and *taking note* of its outcome through which the East Timorese people expressed their clear wish to begin a process of transition under the authority of the United Nations towards independence, which it regards as an accurate reflection of the views of the East Timorese people,

...

Reaffirming the need for all parties to ensure that the rights of refugees and displaced persons are protected, and that they are able to return voluntarily in safety and security to their homes,

Reaffirming respect for the sovereignty and territorial integrity of Indonesia,

Noting the importance of ensuring the security of the boundaries of East Timor, and *noting* in this regard the expressed intention of the Indonesian authorities to cooperate with the multinational force deployed pursuant to resolution 1264 (1999) and with the United Nations Transitional Administration in East Timor,

...

Determining that the continuing situation in East Timor constitutes a threat to peace and security,

Acting under Chapter VII of the Charter of the United Nations,

1. *Decides* to establish, in accordance with the report of the Secretary-General, a United Nations Transitional Administration in East Timor (UNTAET), which will be endowed with overall responsibility for the administration of East Timor and will be empowered to exercise all legislative and executive authority, including the administration of justice;

2. *Decides also* that the mandate of UNTAET shall consist of the following elements:

(*a*) To provide security and maintain law and order throughout the territory of East Timor;

(*b*) To establish an effective administration;

(*c*) To assist in the development of civil and social services;

(*d*) To ensure the coordination and delivery of humanitarian assistance, rehabilitation and development assistance;

(*e*) To support capacity-building for self-government;

(*f*) To assist in the establishment of conditions for sustainable development;

3. *Decides further* that UNTAET will have objectives and a structure along the lines set out in part IV of the report of the Secretary-General, and in particular that its main components will be:

(*a*) A governance and public administration component, including an international police element with a strength of up to 1,640 officers;

(*b*) A humanitarian assistance and emergency rehabilitation component;

(*c*) A military component, with a strength of up to 8,950 troops and up to 200 military observers;

4. *Authorizes* UNTAET to take all necessary measures to fulfil its mandate;

5. *Recognizes* that, in developing and performing its functions under its mandate, UNTAET will need to draw on the expertise and capacity of Member States, United Nations agencies and other international organizations, including the international financial institutions;

6. *Welcomes* the intention of the Secretary-General to appoint a Special Representative who, as the Transitional Administrator, will be responsible for all aspects of the United Nations work in East Timor and will have the power to enact new laws and regulations and to amend, suspend or repeal existing ones;

7. *Stresses* the importance of cooperation between Indonesia, Portugal and UNTAET in the implementation of this resolution;

8. *Stresses* the need for UNTAET to consult and cooperate closely with the East Timorese people in order to carry out its mandate effectively with a view to the development of local democratic institutions, including an independent East Timorese human rights institution, and the transfer to these institutions of its administrative and public service functions;

9. *Requests* UNTAET and the multinational force deployed pursuant to resolution 1264 (1999) to cooperate closely with each other, with a view also to the replacement as soon as possible of the multinational force by the military component of UNTAET, as notified by the Secretary-General having consulted the leadership of the multinational force, taking into account conditions on the ground;

10. *Reiterates* the urgent need for coordinated humanitarian and reconstruction assistance, and *calls upon* all parties to cooperate with humanitarian and human rights organizations so as to ensure their safety, the protection of civilians, in particular children, the safe return of refugees and displaced persons and the effective delivery of humanitarian aid;

11. *Welcomes* the commitment of the Indonesian authorities to allow the refugees and displaced persons in West Timor and elsewhere in Indonesia to choose whether to return to East Timor, remain where they are or be resettled in other parts of Indonesia, and *stresses* the importance of allowing full, safe and unimpeded access by humanitarian organizations in carrying out their work;

12. *Stresses* that it is the responsibility of the Indonesian authorities to take immediate and effective measures to ensure the safe return of refugees in West Timor and other parts of Indonesia to East Timor, the security of refugees, and the civilian and humanitarian character of refugee camps and settlements, in particular by curbing the violent and intimidatory activities of the militias there;

. . .

15. *Underlines* the importance of including in UNTAET personnel with appropriate training in international humanitarian, human rights and refugee law, including child and gender-related provisions, negotiation and communication skills, cultural awareness and civilian–military coordination;

16. *Condemns* all violence and acts in support of violence in East Timor, *calls* for their immediate end, and *demands* that those responsible for such violence be brought to justice;

17. *Decides* to establish UNTAET for an initial period until 31 January 2001;

. . .

Source: UN Security Council Resolution 1272, 25 Oct. 1999, available on the UN Internet site at <http://www.un.org/Docs/scres/1999/sc99.htm>.

Appendix B. East Timor and Kosovo: maps and UN missions

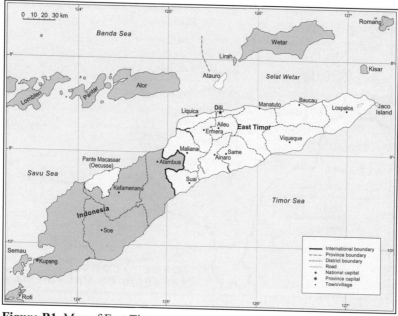

Figure B1. Map of East Timor

Figure B2. Map of Kosovo

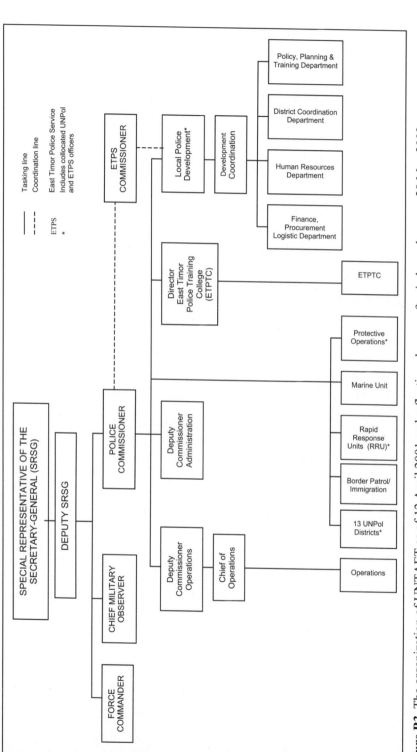

Figure B3. The organization of UNTAET as of 12 April 2001 and reflecting changes after independence on 20 May 2002

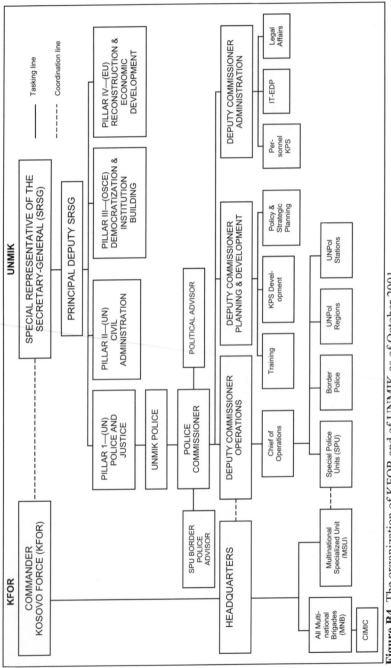

Figure B4. The organization of KFOR and of UNMIK as of October 2001

About the authors

Renata Dwan (Ireland) is leader of the SIPRI Conflict Prevention, Management and Resolution Project and the project on International Policing: the New Agenda, and was previously deputy director of the East–West Institute's European Security Programme. She received her PhD in International Relations from Oxford University. She edited *Building Security in Europe's New Border-lands: Subregional Cooperation in the Wider Europe* (1999), co-edited (with Oleksandr Pavliuk) *Building Security in the New States of Eurasia: Subregional Cooperation in the Former Soviet Space* (2000) and has contributed chapters to the SIPRI Yearbook since joining SIPRI in 1999. At the time this book was completed she was on leave to serve as special adviser to the EU Police Mission in Bosnia and Herzegovina (EUPM) Planning Team in the secretariat of the Council of the European Union.

Michael J. Dziedzic (USA) is a retired colonel of the US Air Force and a graduate of the US Air Force Academy. He joined the United States Institute of Peace (USIP) in 2001 as a programme officer in the Balkans Initiative, and before that was a senior military fellow at the Institute for National Strategic Studies. He received his PhD in Government from the University of Texas at Austin. His 30-year career with the US Air Force included service as tenured professor in the Political Science Department at the US Air Force Academy, as professor of national security studies at the National War College and as a strategic military planner for the UN Mission in Kosovo, and he has been a visiting fellow at the International Institute for Strategic Studies (IISS) in London. Among his publications are *Policing the New World Disorder: Peace Operations and Public Security* (co-edited with Robert Oakley, 1998) and *Mexico: Converging Challenges* (1989).

Annika S. Hansen (Norway) is a senior scientist at the Norwegian Defence Research Establishment (FFI) working on peacekeeping issues, including public security and military–police cooperation in peace operations. A former Fulbright scholar, she was a research associate at the IISS, where she wrote an Adelphi Paper entitled *From Congo to Kosovo: Civilian Police in Peace Operations* (2002). She holds an MA and a PhD in Political Science from the University of Oslo and an MALD from the Fletcher School of Law and Diplomacy, Medford, Mass.

Eirin Mobekk (Norway) is currently a lecturer in security studies at the Department of Peace Studies, University of Bradford, working on security sector reform—more specifically police and judicial reform and UN peace operations, focusing particularly on civil society and its perspectives. Part of her post-doctoral work was a study on the UN civilian police operation in East Timor. Her PhD thesis, at the Department of War Studies, King's College, London, focused on the UN-sponsored military intervention in Haiti in 1994, discussing factors such as disarmament, the abolition of the army, the creation of the new police force, democratization and the issues of justice and reconciliation, and examining the perspective of Haitians.

Robert M. Perito (USA) is an adjunct professor in the Program on Peace-keeping Policy at George Mason University and Senior Fellow at the USIP, and was formerly deputy director of the International Criminal Investigative Training Assistance Program (ICITAP) at the US Department of Justice, where he was responsible for providing policy guidance and programme direction for ICITAP training programmes for indigenous and international police in peace operations. This involved oversight of programmes covering the peacekeeping environments in Bosnia, Kosovo and East Timor and in the post-conflict environments in Albania, Croatia and Macedonia. For over 25 years he was a Foreign Service officer with the US Department of State. He holds an MA in peace operations policy from George Mason University.

Colette Rausch (USA) specializes in rule-of-law issues in peace operations in the USIP. Before joining the USIP she served with the Organization for Security and Co-operation in Europe (OSCE) in Kosovo as director of the Department of Human Rights and Rule of Law, and before that was a federal prosecutor with the US Department of Justice, prosecuting cases which included racketeering and money laundering. She was detailed for six months to Bosnia to work on various criminal justice projects; worked in Hungary on an organized crime task force development project; and during her last year at the Department of Justice was Program Manager for Central and East Europe, establishing prosecutorial development and training projects in Albania, Bosnia, Croatia, Kosovo and Macedonia. She received her Juris Doctorate from Santa Clara University School of Law, and her BA from the University of Nevada, Reno.

Eric Scheye (Germany/USA) was for two years policy and planning officer in the Civilian Police Division of the UN Department of Peace-keeping Operations. Among other responsibilities, he wrote the United Nations *Civilian Police Principles and Guidelines* (draft 2000, published in 2001), and edited and contributed to the chapter on the public security sector of the forthcoming *Multi-Dimensional Peacekeeping Handbook*. He worked for three years in Bosnia and Herzegovina, was a visiting professor at Potsdam University and holds a PhD and MBA. He is currently public security sector reform adviser for the United Nations Development Programme (UNDP) Bureau for Crisis Prevention and Recovery.

Index